STEP-BY-STEP JOURNEY

JHANA
TRAINING
MANUAL

HOW TO GO BEYOND MINDFULNESS
ON MEDITATION RETREATS

Tomas Piskacek

Title: Jhana Training Manual: Step-by-Step Journey from Mindfulness to Cessation

Author: Tomáš Piskáček

Publisher: Tomáš Piskáček, Šestajovice, Czech Republic

Producer: Amazon Kindle Direct Publishing, Seattle, WA, USA; 2025

First edition, April 2025, version 1.0

Cover and interior design: Miblart

Website: www.jhana.training

Passages from the *Sutta Pitaka* translations are reprinted with kind permission from Wisdom Publications.

You can contact the author via the contact form at www.jhana.training

ISBN 978-80-11-06660-4 (paperback)

ISBN 978-80-11-06661-1 (hardcover)

ISBN 978-80-11-06663-5 (ePub)

ISBN 978-80-11-06664-2 (kpf)

ISBN 978-80-11-06665-9 (mp3)

Foreword

Are the Jhanas and states beyond truly within reach? It depends. With the right guidance, patience, and dedication, the answer is yes. This manual is for serious meditators seeking to cultivate profound states of concentration and bliss within the focused environment of a retreat.

Drawing from both early Buddhist texts and practical experience, this book offers:

- Practical retreat guidelines to optimize one's meditation schedule
- Step-by-step instructions for developing deep Samadhi
- Strategies to overcome common obstacles in concentration practice

Whether embarking on a silent retreat or refining one's mindfulness practice at home, this guide serves as a trusted companion on the path to deeper stillness—laying a strong foundation for the development of wisdom.

This is the book I wish I had when I began my journey 30 years ago.

Venerable Ariyadhammika Mahathera
Leader of the Sangha of SBS Monk
Training Centre, Malaysia

Perspectives from Meditation Researchers

The Jhana Training Manual provides a comprehensive and no-nonsense introduction to the practice of jhana. The book avoids theoretical discussion, and yet draws on recent research on jhana. This creates a balanced presentation of the jhanas while focusing on how to actually experience these profound states of blissful peace.

Tomas shares some unique "tricks of the trade" that may help open up access to jhana. The writing is straightforward and represents condensed wisdom. There are also numerous interesting phenomenological details on how both jhana and cessation unfold. Indeed, the parts on the cessation of perception and feeling should not be underestimated.

The book contains complete instructions for one way of entry into nirvana—I can recommend it with the greatest confidence.

Terje Sparby, PhD
Professor of Philosophy and Meditation Researcher
Oslo, Norway

The *Jhana Training Manual* is a rare and masterful contribution to the landscape of contemporary meditation literature. Tomas Piskacek brings precision, humility, and lived insight to one of the most elusive and misunderstood areas of contemplative practice. This manual is not merely theoretical—it is forged in the crucible of deep retreat, rigorous training, and hard-won personal realization. Grounded in the early Buddhist suttas, yet refreshingly practical and accessible, it offers clear, methodical guidance for meditators seeking to traverse the full arc of deep absorptive practice.

Whether you are a beginning practitioner or an advanced contemplative, this manual provides indispensable tools for unlocking the depths of the human mind and heart.

David R. Vago, PhD
President, International Society for Contemplative Research

This is called the bliss of renunciation, the bliss of seclusion, the bliss of peace, the bliss of enlightenment. I say of this kind of pleasure that it should be pursued, that it should be developed, that it should be cultivated, that it should not be feared.

The Buddha on the four jhanas
The Middle Length Discourses of the Buddha, sutta 66

Table of Contents

This manual includes practical advice for the following meditation practices:

TABLE OF MEDITATION TECHNIQUES/ATTAINMENTS

Type	Attainment	Meditation Technique/ Attainment
Mindfulness	0	Walking
		Long/short breath awareness
		Experiencing the whole body
		Tranquilizing the bodily formation
Jhana	1	First jhana
	2	Second jhana
	3	Third jhana
	4	Fourth jhana
Formless (absorption)	5	Infinite space
	6	Infinite consciousness
	7	Nothingness
	8	Neither perception nor non-perception
No conscious experience	9	Cessation of perception and feeling (Nirodha samapatti)

Introduction

About the manual

What is it?

This manual provides comprehensive practical guidance for developing the jhanas (profoundly serene and blissful states of meditative concentration), potentially all the way to the cessation of perception and feeling (*nirodha samapatti*)—the highest meditative attainment possible according to the early Buddhist scriptures. The basis for developing the jhanas is the practice of mindfulness of breathing. The guidance is based on my personal experience with all the meditative states discussed in the manual.

The early Buddhist texts are the scriptural basis for the meditative states—the nine attainments (four jhanas, four formless attainments, and the cessation of perception and feeling). Specifically, it's the *Sutta Pitaka*[1]—the "suttas" (for the sake of simplicity and consistency with the quoted suttas, I omit diacritics for the Pali[2] terms; the Pali terms are in italics, except for the frequently used terms "jhana," "samadhi," and "sutta").

---

[1] "Basket of Discourses"—canonical texts of Theravada Buddhism.
[2] The language of the Theravada canonical texts.

1

However, even the suttas say that the Buddha himself learned to enter some of the states (the seventh and eighth attainments of the nine) before awakening from other ascetics.[3] That means these meditative states are not reserved for Buddhists only and can be practiced separately from the Buddha's teaching. I aim to provide practical advice on developing the meditative states, not to delve into the Buddha's doctrine beyond what is necessary for the meditation training. Whether it is used secularly or as part of the Buddhist Eightfold Path is up to the reader.

I include the most relevant information that may help progress towards and through the nine meditative attainments. The manual focuses on mind training in a retreat setting, covering both the time on and off the meditation cushion. I do not claim that following the approach here will make everyone enter the jhanas. I do claim, though, that if met with some other factors (see the Theory chapter for details), it can lead one all the way from mindfulness, through the jhanas and formless attainments, to the cessation of perception and feeling—*nirodha samapatti*.

Who is it for?

The manual is suitable for anyone (laypeople, monks, or nuns) aspiring to go beyond basic mindfulness on a meditation retreat. Beginners can start by practicing mindfulness of breathing as described here at home and use it as a basis for their first meditation retreat in the future. Intermediate

---

[3] *The Middle Length Discourses of the Buddha*, sutta 26.

practitioners with retreat experience can use the tips here to fine-tune their training and progress further. Expert meditators already mastering the formless attainments can see whether the tips for getting from the neither perception nor non-perception to the cessation of perception and feeling will work.

The training is tailored to developing deeper meditative states on a retreat. However, if you do not plan to go on a meditation retreat, you can still use the mindfulness of breathing techniques for your mind practice outside of a retreat setting.

The manual does not take into account the potential mental health issues of the meditator. I don't have any professional education in that area. The instructions assume the meditator is generally in good health. For such individuals, I'm not aware of any potential health risks associated with the practices described here. If you have a relevant health condition, it is advisable to discuss the suitability of attending a meditation retreat with a healthcare professional.

Why did I write it?

The nine meditative attainments have changed my life. These states cannot compare to anything experienceable in everyday life. Calling them the utmost meditative bliss, peace, and release is not an exaggeration. I want to make them more accessible to others—that is my mission. The training is not easy, and making it to jhana is not guaranteed. But it's undoubtedly worth trying.

Overview of chapters

PART 1: GROUNDWORK FOR SERENITY

- **Chapter 1—Theory**: *Clarifies the key terms used throughout the manual and discusses the key factors for attaining jhana.*

- **Chapter 2—Training Outside of Meditation**: *Covers all relevant aspects of the meditation retreat practice outside of formal meditation, including a suggested daily retreat schedule.*

- **Chapter 3—General Meditation Tips**: *Practical advice relating to any level of meditation.*

- **Chapter 4—Mindfulness Training**: *Provides meditation instruction for three modes of mindfulness of breathing, the third one potentially culminating in the first jhana. Includes a table with an overview of the mindfulness of breathing techniques.*

PART 2: ADVANCED MEDITATION

- **Chapter 5—Jhana Training**: *Walks the reader through the practice of the four jhanas, lists their benefits, and provides a table summarizing the jhana practice. Realistic timeframes for getting into the jhanas are also discussed.*

- **Chapter 6—Beyond Jhana: Formless Attainments**: *Explains the meaning of the "formless," provides* *instruction for transitioning from the fourth jhana to the formless absorption, and continues the journey through the meditative attainments to the edge of conscious experience.*

- **Chapter 7—Cessation of Perception and Feeling (Nirodha Samapatti)**: *Detailed elaboration of the highest meditative state, including tips for attaining it, my first experience of emerging from it, some features and effects of the cessation practice (e.g., nonduality), and ways to check for oneself that the cessation is happening.*

- **Chapter 8—General Notes**: *Closes the meditation discussion with final thoughts and tips on the samadhi[4] training, especially on overestimation.*

- *Each chapter ends with a few key takeaways.* **Summary of Key Takeaways** *follows the* **Conclusion** *of the manual.*

Chapters 2–4 will be the most practical for most meditating readers. Part 2 (chapters 5–8) deals with advanced mind training requiring more extended retreat periods. Therefore, Part 1 (chapters 1–4) will suffice for mindfulness practitioners who are unconcerned about the advanced meditation stages. Finally, chapter 7—Cessation of Perception and Feeling— might be the most interesting for readers curious about advanced meditation, as accurate information on the cessation attainment is scarce.

---

[4] Unification of mind, one-pointedness of mind; the next chapter explains the term in more detail.

Who is the author of the methods described in the manual?

The approach described here is my method in the sense that it's how I've practiced and what has worked for me. But it's not my method in the sense that I would be the sole original author of it. It is based on the suttas; I learned most of the meditation instructions from my teacher—Venerable Ariyadhammika Mahathera; some things are probably common knowledge in the Theravada meditation circles, passed on to me by others, and the rest are my inventions.

Some of the tips may seem obvious to experienced meditators. I still include them as the aim is to provide a comprehensive manual helpful to beginners and advanced practitioners alike.

About the author

My name is Tomas. I was born in Prague, the Czech Republic, in 1987. I grew up playing tennis (and I see some parallels between training to be a professional athlete and training to attain the most profound states in meditation). I studied economics and public policy at Kenyon College (BA, Ohio), the London School of Economics, and the University of Amsterdam (MSc). Among my few jobs, I spent the longest time at McKinsey & Company in Prague as a research analyst. I also enjoyed teaching economics part-time at a high school.

I became interested in Buddhism when I was 16 and started meditating at 18—about 20 years ago. During my studies and work, I sometimes meditated at home and used to go to a 10–14-day retreat once a year, usually with Bhante Sujiva as a teacher (Mahasi meditation method).

At the end of 2018, I went to Sasanarakkha Buddhist Sanctuary in Malaysia to become a Theravada monk under the guidance of Venerable Ariyadhammika. At that time, I didn't consider myself an especially good meditator. Long sits were uncomfortable for me (hip and knee pain), I tended to think a lot (one of my past teachers put me in the "obsessive thinkers" category), and after a few days of retreat, my mind was easily overcome by lust. The beginnings at Sasanarakkha were no different.

However, quite unexpectedly, I was able to get into the jhanas and even the formless attainments relatively quickly. Later, in 2022, again at Sasanarakkha, I managed to break through into the cessation of perception and feeling. After that, I maintained and developed the cessation practice for over two years.

Besides Malaysia, I have practiced meditation in Buddhist monasteries in Burma, Thailand, Sri Lanka, and Singapore.

At the end of 2024, I decided to abandon formal monasticism, return to Europe, continue my meditation practice without the monk robes, and dedicate myself to helping others on the path to jhana. I could not do it the same way as a monk since monks are not allowed to report their attainments to laypeople. Also, I delight in forest seclusion and the cessation of perception and feeling, but I cannot say the same about formal monasticism.

I don't expect all the information in the manual to be useful for everyone. But I believe most readers aspiring for the jhanas will find some valuable tips here. Sometimes, the game changers are relatively minor things. Read on to find out what the little trick was for me to break through into the cessation of perception and feeling.

Key Takeaways

*   "This manual provides comprehensive practical guidance
    for developing the jhanas (profoundly serene and blissful
    states of meditative concentration), potentially all the
    way to the cessation of perception and feeling (*nirodha
    samapatti*)—the highest meditative attainment possible
    according to the early Buddhist scriptures."

*   "The manual focuses on mind training in a retreat setting,
    covering both the time on and off the meditation cushion."

*   "The manual is suitable for anyone (laypeople, monks,
    or nuns) aspiring to go beyond basic mindfulness on a
    meditation retreat."

PART 1:
GROUNDWORK
FOR SERENITY

Theory

What do I mean by "jhana," "absorption," and "samadhi"?

Those familiar with the topic of jhanas probably know that there are several understandings of what jhana means. My aim here is not to engage in an extensive theoretical discussion and argue in favor of one of the jhana interpretations. However, clarifying what type of jhana I'm talking about and what I mean by "absorption" is necessary before using these terms in the manual.

First, the scriptural basis I work with is the Bhikkhu Bodhi translations of the suttas. In the suttas, the attainments number five to eight are not called "jhanas," and I also don't think of them as jhanas. I use "formless attainments." You may see the labels I use for the nine attainments in the **Table of Meditation Techniques/Attainments** at the beginning of the manual.

Which "jhana" am I talking about?

I've heard mostly about the classification of jhanas into three types. One such classification is in the book *The Mind Illuminated* (Yates, Immergut and Graves 2017). Another one is in the paper "Toward a Unified Account of Advanced Concentrative Absorption Meditation: A Systematic Definition and Classification of Jhāna" (Sparby and Sacchet 2024). I'm not sure if it's a perfect match, but of the three types—let's call them "lite," "intermediate," and "absorption" jhanas—the jhanas I talk about are closest to the intermediate type. They are not absorption; they are based on the suttas and are the more difficult and profound ones of the sutta-based types[5].

Absorption as the main difference between jhana and the formless

By meditative absorption in its pure form, I mean a state in which one does not perceive through the five senses (one does not feel the body, does not hear or visualize anything, etc.), and the mind is fully absorbed in the perception of its mental object (e.g., infinite space). The state is thus purely mental, immaterial, "unplugged" from any external input.

Exactly that, as I understand it, is the main difference between the four jhanas and the formless attainments. The four jhanas are not absorption, while the formless attainments are. The sutta passage for the base of infinite space describes a

---

[5] The lite and intermediate types are based on the suttas, whereas the absorption type is based on the *Visuddhimagga*.

transition from a non-absorbed state (fourth jhana) into an absorbed state (infinite space):

" . . . *with the complete surmounting of perceptions of form, with the disappearance of perceptions of sensory impact, with non-attention to perceptions of diversity, aware that 'space is infinite,' we enter upon and abide in the base of infinite space.*"[6] (*The Middle Length Discourses of the Buddha*, sutta 31)

The suttas talk about the formless states as "*liberations that are peaceful and immaterial, transcending forms*" (*The Middle Length Discourses of the Buddha*, sutta 70). It refers to being temporarily liberated from form, matter, and the five-sense experience. In the case of infinite space, for instance, the only thing one is aware of, the only thing that is being experienced, is simply infinite space. There is a clear perception of boundless space all around and nothing else.

The mind in absorption is very stable, imperturbable, as if "fixed" or "locked-in." It's not blissful in the sense that there would be a pleasurable feeling (such as in the first three jhanas). The feeling is, technically speaking, neither painful nor pleasant—neutral. It is not an ecstatic bliss. It is a bliss of stability, peace, and freedom from matter and all sensory impact.

Given the jhana sutta similes that talk about pervading the whole body by something (the similes are presented in the Jhana Training chapter), I find it difficult to interpret the four

---

[6] © 2009 by Bhikkhu Bodhi, *The Middle Length Discourses of the Buddha.* Reprinted by arrangement with Wisdom Publications. This attribution applies to all excerpts from *The Middle Length Discourses of the Buddha* throughout the manual.

jhanas as absorptions in which one does not experience the physical body.

I elaborate more on all the meditative attainments in their respective subchapters. Here, I'm clarifying which interpretation of jhana I'm talking about and what I refer to when talking about absorption, which is the main quality differentiating the formless attainments from the jhanas.

What do I mean by "samadhi"?

The term "samadhi" is widespread in meditative circles. The sutta translations I read usually translate it as "concentration," and it often occurs in the context of "*samma-samadhi*"—"right concentration," which is the eighth factor of the Buddhist Noble Eightfold Path defined as the four jhanas.

The suttas also speak about samadhi as "unification of mind," or "one-pointedness of mind."[7] The way I understand it is not that the object of concentration is necessarily one specific point but rather that the mind goes in one direction; it is collected instead of scattered. In that sense, it might also be thought of as "one-directedness of mind."

"Samadhi" is a broader term than "jhana." Jhana is samadhi, but not all samadhi is jhana. The formless attainments are not jhana (unless you use the "eight jhanas" commentarial terminology),

---

[7] *The Middle Length Discourses of the Buddha*, sutta 44.

but they are samadhi. If you're not yet in jhana but are getting close to it, it's probably fair to say you have decent samadhi. This whole manual is about developing samadhi, the jhanas being a specific form of it.

What is the relationship between mindfulness and samadhi, including jhana?

"*Unification of mind, friend Visakha, is concentration [samadhi]; the four foundations[8] of mindfulness are the basis of concentration.*" (*The Middle Length Discourses of the Buddha*, sutta 44)

Mindfulness is a condition for samadhi. It's what precedes and leads to samadhi. In this manual, mindfulness of breathing is the tool for getting into the first jhana—a specific stage of samadhi. In all the lists of certain qualities in the suttas that include both mindfulness (*sati*) and samadhi—such as the five faculties, the seven enlightenment factors, and the Noble Eightfold Path—mindfulness comes before samadhi (and the lists can be seen as a sequence).

Cultivating samadhi is going beyond mindfulness, but it doesn't mean you leave mindfulness behind. Mindfulness is highly developed in the jhanas. The fourth jhana has "purification of mindfulness."[9] If you want the purest mindfulness, go for the jhanas.

---

[8] Body, feelings, mind, mind-objects.
[9] *The Numerical Discourses of the Buddha*, sutta 5.28.

Four key factors for attaining jhana

Developing jhana is learning a new skill—producing a particular altered state of mind at will. Sometimes, meditation is seen as something religious or mystical. I don't think about it that way. I think of it as simply training one's mind and brain. As people go to the gym to train their bodies, similarly, we meditate to train our minds and brains. The jhanas are whole-body experiences, but the main thing is clearly happening and felt in the head.

The factors for developing this new skill—jhana—are not too different from developing other skills. I grew up playing tennis. It's a simplification, but I think it's fair to say that to become a successful tennis player, you need four things:

- Favorable external conditions
- Good coach teaching the proper technique and other aspects of the game
- Persistent effort
- Talent

The key factors for attaining jhana are the same. In a broader sense, they are the four key factors for developing samadhi. Let's dive into them one by one.

Favorable external (retreat) conditions

This one should be more or less clear to those with a solid meditation retreat experience. Generally, the retreat place should be conducive to calming the mind, relatively simple, but not necessarily uncomfortable. Ideally, it would be a quiet, secluded place in nature. It could be a monastery, a retreat center, or an individual lodging.

Silence

The sounds of nature (anyone who has been to a tropical rainforest knows what I'm talking about) are not as much of an issue as human-produced sounds, such as traffic, music, construction work, or other people talking. But generally, the quieter, the better.

Seclusion

Secluded means you're not seeing or meeting other people frequently. If you can get a lodging where you can't see anything other than nature when looking around, that's perfect. But things don't always need to be perfect. If you can get a place where you're not disturbed by noise or other people, that will do.

Simplicity

I mentioned that the place should be simple. As I will explain later, the "job" will be calming the mind in meditation and not distracting it outside of it. Keeping the place simple means avoiding things that may distract the mind. In a way, the retreat place should be boring. Bring only things you will really need. The retreat activities only include sleeping, eating, meditating, contemplating, being out in nature, and maybe reading, exercising, and discussing the training with someone else.

Moderate comfort

In terms of level of comfort, balance is the way to go. Some meditators resort to very ascetic conditions, which is OK but not necessary for developing jhana. Luxury doesn't help either. The simplicity should make it less comfortable than what you're used to in your non-retreat setting. You can push yourself a bit. But you should not suffer too much.

Supportive diet

Food is also a thing to consider when planning a retreat. Having enough energy and feeling well helps the mind training. Try to make sure you are somewhere where you can get enough healthy, nutritious "fuel" for the training.

The more time, the better

I also include time in this external conditions factor. It's straightforward—the more time you have for the retreat, the better. If you can get two weeks, that would be good. One month, great. Two to three months, samadhi through the roof. Maybe. Even if you can get only a week or a weekend, it's worth it. You will not attain jhana, but that's OK. It's a gradual training. Every meditation counts. Regularly meditating outside the retreat setting and going on a short retreat occasionally means starting from a higher base when you eventually do find the time for a more extended retreat.

Group or solitary retreat?

The loneliness of a solitary retreat can have both advantages and disadvantages. The advantage is that you can be more secluded and less disturbed by others, and you can tailor the daily schedule to yourself. The disadvantage is that loneliness may be challenging, especially for beginners. If you prefer a group retreat, try to find one with a conducive set-up and environment for developing jhana. If you prefer a solitary retreat, don't underestimate the challenge of being alone. Feeding yourself measured doses of friendly human interaction, ideally with someone you can discuss the practice with, is advisable.

Good instruction and advice

Good instruction and advice are essential. Just as with learning other skills, the right advice at the right time can save plenty of time and make the difference between mediocre and good results. So, where, or from whom, can you get the right meditation instruction and advice? A million-dollar question.

In the spiritual circles, you get a wide range of figures, from con artists who fake their "enlightenments," through people who, with genuinely good intentions, preach things that hardly make sense, to wise teachers worth following. There is no universal magic formula for telling one from another. *Jhana Training Manual* would be a simple answer to the million-dollar question, indeed, but a slightly biased one coming from the author of it.

I had a couple of pages written on selecting a teacher. However, I will abstain from sharing it. I think it's fairer to recuse myself from commenting on the topic in detail since I myself offer meditation advice and instruction.

Generally speaking, when choosing the person and method to follow, it's good to invest time in one's own research into the matter, be careful about confirmation bias, be skeptical about methods promising quick results, avoid blindly accepting recommendations of others, and be open to adjusting if you realize there might be a better way than your current method.

Persistent effort

Don't focus on things you cannot control, such as the results. Focus on things you can influence, such as your persistent effort.

This factor is solely up to you. No one can do the work for you. Even with the best external conditions and instruction, it won't work without some striving. It's closely related to motivation and mindset.

I don't believe much in artificial motivation boosting. You're either genuinely interested, or you're not. If you are and have the conditions for the training, go all in. I like the term "wholeheartedly." I have no doubt it's worth it, whether you make it to jhana or not. If you do, it will change your life. If you don't, you have increased the chance of it happening the next time.

By the way, even the pre-jhanic states can be very rewarding. It's not an all-or-nothing game whether you get to jhana or not.

It's rather about whether you play (go to a retreat) or not. If you do, you always win at least something. If not jhana, it may be the pre-jhanic pleasantness and peace of mind. If nothing else, you spent some quiet time developing mindfulness and tranquility in nature.

Talent

Talent is not at all the most important thing. But it is a thing. In many areas of skill development—sports, arts, professional work, and others—there are cases of people having similar starting conditions and training methods, putting in a similar amount of effort, and the results being quite different. Samadhi development is no different.

To what extent talent is inborn or determined in our childhood and by our upbringing is not relevant to our discussion. For this manual, let's define talent as the "inner potential for samadhi we cannot influence."

I think teachers, coaches, motivational speakers, and the like, sometimes underplay the role of talent. Putting significant weight on talent is inconvenient because it may sound discouraging. Again, I'm far from saying that talent is the leading factor. However, omitting it from the key factors would be inconsistent with reality. It would lead to the expectation that if one does everything correctly, the jhanas must happen. Unfortunately, that's not how it works. Due to this talent factor, I cannot promise anyone that the jhanas will happen.

A crucial thing to add is that you cannot know whether you have the talent until you try. By trying, I mean fulfilling the three previous factors on a longer retreat. If you go on a short retreat and don't experience anything special, it doesn't mean you don't have the talent.

I remember quitting early twice on two-week retreats before I became a monk. I couldn't handle it and left the retreats after a week or so. Even if you're struggling on relatively short retreats, it doesn't imply you don't have the talent for samadhi and the potential for jhana.

Struggling with the hindrances at the beginning is normal. The trick is to get through that difficult initial period while cultivating samadhi. Then, if the samadhi grows, it will subdue the hindrances, and suddenly everything becomes much more manageable.

So, please, don't get into that "can't do" attitude before giving it a serious try on a long retreat. The (un)realistic timeframes for attaining jhana—that is, what I mean by a long retreat—are discussed in the Jhana Training chapter.

Overall, you don't need all four factors to be perfect, but you do need all of them to some degree to get to jhana. The first one—favorable external (retreat) conditions—is a matter of arrangement. The third one—persistent effort—is up to you. We can't do anything about the fourth one—talent. You need to try and see what happens. And yes, the whole purpose of this manual is to get you covered regarding that second factor—good instruction and advice.

Key Takeaways

* " . . . of the three types—let's call them 'lite,' 'intermediate' and 'absorption' jhanas—the jhanas I talk about are closest to the intermediate type."

* "Exactly that [absorption], as I understand it, is the main difference between the four jhanas and the formless attainments. The four jhanas are not absorption, while the formless attainments are."

* "Cultivating samadhi is going beyond mindfulness, but it doesn't mean you leave mindfulness behind. Mindfulness is highly developed in the jhanas. . . . If you want the purest mindfulness, go for the jhanas."

* The four key factors for attaining jhana are:

    • Favorable external (retreat) conditions
    • Good instruction and advice
    • Persistent effort
    • Talent

* "Don't focus on things you cannot control, such as the results. Focus on things you can influence, such as your persistent effort."

2

Training Outside of Meditation

What (not) to do when you are not meditating

Developing samadhi on a retreat is the art of calming and unifying the mind in meditation and not ruining it outside of it. Let's start with the "not ruining it" part.

Samadhi killers

Some activities that are normal, at least for laypeople, outside of retreat, need to be minimized or completely avoided for samadhi to flourish. Generally, these are the activities that excite and stir the mind in one way or another.

At the beginning of the training, when samadhi is not yet developed, and the mind is unsettled, the negative effect of such activities may not seem so apparent. That's because you don't experience the contrast between less and more samadhi when there is no samadhi. But as samadhi gains ground, it's easy to see how these activities weaken it (sooner or later, you will likely experience them and see it, except for the third one, which should not be tested in order to see it, of course). I call them "samadhi killers." They are:

- Using electronic devices
- Conversations
- Any sexual activity
- Anger, irritation

Using electronic devices

This refers to using a laptop, tablet, smartphone, or similar device for virtually anything: messaging, browsing the internet, reading the news, listening to music, and so on. Watching videos is even worse than reading. Try to minimize these things as much as possible.

You may not be able to get it down to zero. Maybe you need to send a message that you cannot postpone, or something like that. That's OK. You don't necessarily need to go into full medieval-age offline mode. But try to limit it to things that are unavoidable.

The ideal amount is zero though. And spending a few hours a day using an electronic device ruins the retreat (at least from the perspective of developing samadhi).

Conversations

You can hardly completely avoid this one, and it's not even the goal. The ideal amount of talking to others is little, not zero.

You will probably need to get food somewhere and interact with others. There may be a practice discussion from time to time. If on a group retreat, you may need to sort out some logistics with others. That's all fine. There is no need to observe complete silence and act deaf when someone talks to you. Actually, after some time on a retreat, it can gladden and help the mind to have a brief friendly conversation.

Generally, try to minimize it to what is necessary and protect your quiet space. If someone disturbs you by talking to you more than you'd like, avoid the person or try to explain the situation to sort it out.

Any sexual activity

Terrible, I know. This may be the most challenging one for many meditators. I discuss it in more detail in the chapter dealing with hindrances. Again, it may not seem it should make much difference. But indeed, for fulfilling the samadhi potential, refraining from sexual pleasures is important.

Anger, irritation

This doesn't refer just to some dislike or minor frustration. It refers to the anger that makes you "boil" inside—a beautiful samadhi killer. A detailed discussion of it is also part of the hindrances subchapter.

Activities you cannot avoid: sleeping, eating, thinking

Sleeping

Sometimes, sleeping less on retreats is considered a good practice. Some meditators tend to show off by how little they sleep. Indeed, when you get to jhana, you can function with less sleep than usual. The mind is bright, fresh, energized, and doesn't tire easily.

However, when not yet in jhana, purely from a samadhi development perspective, I don't see any benefit in pushing oneself to sleep less than usual. Getting enough sleep to be fresh and well-rested for the meditation practice is important. It's also OK to get a nap during the day.

How many hours of sleep per day people need is individual; you need to figure that out for yourself. Don't oversleep; don't undersleep.

Eating

Eating little is sometimes part of the retreat experience. Generally, I don't disagree with that approach. But this manual is attempting to be a pragmatic guide for developing samadhi. For that purpose, limiting energy intake may not always be optimal.

When on a retreat and samadhi is not yet developed, usually less food is needed as the retreat schedule is not very energy-demanding. That may change with getting to the jhanas and higher. The extent is probably individual. My experience with the meditative attainments is that they are highly energy-demanding. Especially the states beyond jhana—absorptions. As discussed earlier, these states are subjectively purely mental. But in a way, they are pretty physical. As I understand it, the brain needs a lot of fuel to produce and maintain them for hours.

So, how do you approach eating on a jhana retreat? I suggest a balance. If you want to prioritize getting into the jhanas, I don't think trying to be ascetic and eating little is helpful (but I'm not saying it's impossible to get to jhana while eating little). On the other hand, overeating doesn't help either.

The optimal practice is to eat the amount of food that gives you enough energy for the mind training, but not more than that. The optimal amount of food for the practice may change during the retreat. You may need more if you get into the deeper stages of samadhi.

There is no choice if you're bound by rules prohibiting eating after midday (e.g., if you're a Theravada monk, nun, or an eight-precept follower). If such rules do not bind you, don't worry about fasting in the afternoon and evening; it's not necessary for the jhana training. Within the approach of not overeating, but getting enough energy for the practice, feel free to eat whenever you need. A lack of energy does not help samadhi.

Thinking

Sometimes there is a misunderstanding that thinking per se is a problem. It's not. From the nine meditative attainments

31

perspective, unless you're in the second jhana or higher, there is always some thinking, and that's all right.

The thing to work with is what you're thinking about. Thoughts stirring up anger will hurt your samadhi. Contemplating the training may help you a lot. You need to think to learn from mistakes and fine-tune the training process. By the way, contemplation can be a good *vipassana* (insight) practice (meaning formal meditation is not the only way to develop *vipassana*).

Needless to say, the thinking activity can range from very calm to out-of-control restlessness. The jhanas lead to the former (very calm thinking outside of meditation).

You can work with three categories of thoughts:

- Helpful thoughts:

    These are the thoughts that help along the path, that support you in your training. Without such thoughts, you wouldn't even be on a retreat. Broadly, these can be any thoughts or contemplation related to your "life philosophy" (for Buddhists, that would be thoughts about the *Dhamma*, for example). More narrowly, these are the thoughts related to the meditation retreat training.

    Don't be afraid of such thoughts. Prefer them over any other thoughts.

- Unhelpful thoughts:

This is the "no-no" category. These are any thoughts of sexuality (more generally, sensuality) or anger. It's crucial to add that this category includes seemingly harmless thoughts that have the potential to unfold into direct thoughts of sexuality or anger. I discuss this further in the subchapter on hindrances.

These thoughts are unhelpful because once they unfold, they are difficult to stop, and they complicate the cultivation of serenity of mind. I believe most of those who have been to a meditation retreat know what I'm talking about.

Try to prevent, avoid, and abandon these thoughts. The later you do it, and the more they unfold, the more difficult it is to stop them. And a mind overcome by lust or anger is not close to jhana.

- Neutral thoughts:

These are all the thoughts that don't fall into either of the two previous categories. These could be thoughts about your work, friends, family, plans for the future, and so on. It could be many things. Such thoughts don't help the training, but they usually don't overly harm samadhi as long as they don't evolve into unhelpful thoughts.

A realistic thinking strategy for meditation retreats is to stay as far away as possible from the unhelpful thoughts; prefer the helpful thoughts—if you can be with them, great; and if not, the middle category is also acceptable.

Optional activities: reading, exercising, discussing the training

The last group of activities, after the samadhi "killers," and those you cannot avoid, are optional activities: reading, exercising, and discussing the training with a trusted advisor.

Reading

Reading itself does not help samadhi, naturally. However, it can have a positive effect on the general mindset. Reading something related to the helpful thoughts category about one to two hours a day can inspire and gladden the mind, help in case you're bored, and serve as "food" for (helpful) contemplation. It's much better to get a bit distracted by reading something meaningful and contemplating it than getting under the influence of the unhelpful thoughts out of boredom.

If you want to focus on meditation only, don't find yourself bored, and don't have too much free time, you don't need to read, of course. However, if you do feel bored, maybe even demotivated, try reading something directly or indirectly related to the practice.

This is an exception to not using electronic devices. The same approach applies to listening to audiobooks, Dhamma talks, and the like.

Exercising

Physical exercise is similar to reading in that it doesn't help the mind calm down but can improve general retreat well-being. Feel free to use it in measured doses. A walk in nature for about an hour every day is a good and healthy compromise between not moving at all and throwing your tranquility off with an intense workout.

Discussing the training with a trusted advisor

I intentionally do not use the term "meditation interview." Formal meditation is the main focus, but the "training" refers to virtually everything you do or don't do on the retreat. Discussing training can thus include meditation, dealing with the hindrances outside of meditation, daily schedule, your questions about the theory of the practice, and other things. It should be a holistic approach. A perfect meditation technique won't bear its fruits if appropriate conduct outside of meditation doesn't support it.

I include this point in optional activities because experienced meditators may not need much guidance. However, I would recommend that beginners and intermediate meditators discuss their training, especially when entering unchartered waters, such as applying a new method or going on a more extended retreat than ever before. The frequency of training discussions can be flexible, from every day for beginners, to once a week for the more experienced ones. Or it can be done ad hoc when the need arises.

Talking to another human being can have more benefits than just fine-tuning the practice. After some time on a retreat, especially a solitary one, you may find yourself bored, demotivated, or simply lonely. We are still "social animals." Regular discussions, or just brief check-ins, can help prevent that.

Discussing the training is an exception to trying to minimize conversations.

There are two more topics I want to discuss in this subchapter: boredom and full awareness outside of formal meditation.

Boredom

Among the top issues people struggle with on retreats are sensual desire, irritation toward others, and boredom.

Boredom being on the list makes sense. People are used to being bombarded with external stimuli and seek easy excitement. Then you come on a retreat and cut all that off, or at least minimize it. You are mostly offline. You don't have chitchat with your friends. You seclude yourself from the rest of the world, including the ordinary excitements. You're left with mindful breathing, walking, and the abovementioned activities. Switching to that calm, simple retreat mode probably sounds good if you're tired of a busy life. But sooner or later during the retreat, you can get bored.

Jhana is incredibly blissful. However, the daily routine leading towards it is not super-exciting. And it makes complete sense. It's about calming and unifying the mind and avoiding things that excite it. The jhana bliss comes from seclusion and internal serenity. So, yes, regarding the usual non-meditative excitements, the retreat routine is kind of boring. That boredom can be extremely blissful though. I call it "blissful boredom." It's worth it.

So, how do you deal with boredom? There are two ways that can be combined:

The first is entertaining yourself with something from the optional activities repertoire. You could read something interesting that supports helpful thoughts. You could take a break from meditation and go on a trip in nature. You could also have an extra talk with your training discussion partner or a friend. It's not necessary to rigidly stick to the daily schedule all the time. But be careful not to let these "extras" lead your practice astray.

The second one is accepting boredom as the "cost of samadhi." Having a tranquil mind and a lot of fun simultaneously is impossible. You can't have your cake and eat it too. If you want to have fun, go party. If you want peace of mind and jhana, go on a retreat. So, if the meditation practice is going well, but you feel somewhat bored, just accept it. It's still a good deal;

it's not the worst problem to have. Boredom being the biggest issue on a retreat is a relatively good scenario.

Full awareness outside of formal meditation

Mindfulness has become a big thing in the West. I believe that's a good thing. However, sometimes, the term is overused and inflated.[10] In the context of what you should do outside of the formal meditation sessions, I prefer the term "full awareness" over "mindfulness" (notice I just say "I prefer" it instead of claiming it's the better term to use, which conveniently allows me to dodge explaining why and defining the difference between the two).

What do you do outside of the meditation cushion regarding mindfulness, full awareness, or whatever you call it? As with many other things, balance is the way to go. Try to be fully aware of what you're doing, as opposed to being absent-minded. But I wouldn't consider that meditating.

You don't need to move sloth-speed. You don't need to try to be anxiously mindful every single moment. You don't need to systematically internally label anything. The training is not meditating 24/7.

During the meditation breaks, slow down, be fully aware of what you're doing—be present, prefer the helpful thoughts, try to deal with the hindrances (they will be discussed soon), and avoid the samadhi killers. But also relax, act normal, and

------

[10] For a rigorous discussion related to that topic, see "Mind the Hype: A Critical Evaluation and Prescriptive Agenda for Research on Mindfulness and Meditation" (Van Dam et al. 2017).

smile and enjoy the process if you can. Full awareness will become more and more natural as the mind settles down and mindfulness kicks in in meditation.

Daily schedule

Unless you're on a group retreat, you can tailor the daily schedule to your needs. You can see what works and what doesn't and optimize it. There is no ideal one-size-fits-all schedule. People may have different needs, including the total amount of meditation per day.

Aim for a schedule you can handle for the whole retreat duration without burning out. The first jhana is rapture and bliss. You can hardly get there overstrained.

Regarding the amount of meditation (sitting plus walking), between five and eight hours a day, most of it sitting, will be optimal for most meditators. But if it works for you to be outside of that range, go ahead.

Samadhi is, obviously, positively correlated to how much you meditate. Nevertheless, at a certain point, you hit the ceiling of what you can handle for an extended period. Don't go beyond that. It's better to have a long-term, or, let's say, whole-retreat-term, approach than to overdo it and burn out.

In other words, meditate as much as you can within what you can physically and mentally handle over the whole course of the retreat. By "handle," I don't mean just surviving. I mean not struggling much on account of the amount of meditation. You can push yourself. But you should not suffer.

The meditation sessions should be spread more or less evenly throughout the whole day. Also, aim for consistency in the daily meditation load throughout the retreat.

Here is a suggested daily schedule for five hours of sitting meditation and one to two hours of mindful walking. You can adjust it to your needs and preferences.

DAILY RETREAT SCHEDULE EXAMPLE

Time	Activity
Morning	
5:30	wake up & (optional) cold shower
6-7	**meditation (1)**
7:15-7:45	breakfast
8-9	reading
9-9:30	mindful walking (1)
9:30-10:30	**meditation (2)**
10:45-11:15	training discussion
11:30-12	lunch
Afternoon	
12-13	rest/nap
13-13:30	mindful walking (2)
13:30-14:30	**meditation (3)**
14:30-15:30	light exercise (e.g., a walk in nature)
15:30-16	snack (optional)
16-17	optional (e.g., community service or mindful walking)
17-18	**meditation (4)**

Evening	
18–18:30	snack (optional)
18:30–19	shower, hygiene
19–20	reading/contemplation (e.g., *vipassana*)
20–21	**meditation (5)**
21–22	reading/contemplation (e.g., *vipassana*)
22	bedtime

Dealing with the hindrances

As you get on the retreat, switch to the calmer mode, and abandon most of the external distractions of the non-retreat life, the mind, unfortunately, doesn't automatically follow suit. The mind can be scattered, shaky, full of attachments and passions, and occupied by unending trains of thoughts. It's not natural for the mind to be serene and unified. Going back to the sports comparison, sports skills do not come automatically. You need to train and develop them systematically. The mind training is no different.

The journey from a basic level of mindfulness to the jhana mind is filled with various obstacles. I will be consistent with the classical sutta terminology and call them "hindrances." However, my approach to dealing with them doesn't always entirely copy the traditional one. The approach should be pragmatic, and the yardstick of success should be effectiveness. In other words, use whatever works.

The five hindrances are dullness and drowsiness, doubt, restlessness and remorse, ill will, and sensual desire. It's necessary to overcome the hindrances to attain jhana. The good news is that once you make it to jhana, the jhana will keep the hindrances at bay, even outside of the meditation sessions. In fact, that is one of the main benefits of jhana. Let's look at the hindrances one by one.

Dullness and drowsiness

Many meditators have to deal with this early on at a retreat. In the suttas, a mind oppressed by dullness and drowsiness is compared to water covered by algae and water plants, as opposed to clean water in which you can see your own reflection.[11]

Early on in practice, the mind doesn't have much power to overcome dullness and drowsiness by meditation. I have encountered meditators coming to a retreat tired from their busy lives, being very determined to meditate "hardcore," getting up earlier than they were used to in the morning, and then bravely trying to overcome the drowsiness in meditation. I don't recall any case in which this would work.

From my experience, the most effective are simply the conventional non-meditative remedies: go to bed early, get enough sleep, take a break for a nap if you're falling asleep during meditation, get a cold shower before meditation, exercise a bit, eat light, healthy food, don't overeat, don't

[11] *The Numerical Discourses of the Buddha*, sutta 5.193.

meditate right after your meals, and the like. And then there are the usual caffeine "cheats," of course. As the meditation picks up, it will help further with energy and staying awake.

Overall, dullness and drowsiness are unlikely to be the biggest problem on the path. In the worst case, you unintentionally take a nap during your sitting meditation from time to time—not a tragedy.

Doubt

This refers primarily to doubts about the practice. The suttas compare a mind oppressed by doubt to water that is cloudy, muddy, in darkness.[12]

"Am I doing it right?" "Should I do it this or that way?" "Is it all worth it?" "Who is this Tomas anyway?" Naturally, such questions will arise.

What is the best remedy for doubts about the training? Asking questions, getting answers. There are no secret teachings on the path from mindfulness to the cessation of perception and feeling. Whoever it is, your trusted advisor should be able to answer your questions reasonably. Getting answers (hopefully good ones) to your questions is an integral part of the training that is vital for moving forward.

If no suitable advisor is available, you are left to research, analyze, and test yourself.

---

[12] *The Numerical Discourses of the Buddha*, sutta 5.193.

Restlessness and remorse

This hindrance is compared in the suttas to water stirred by the wind.[13]

The opposite of restlessness is peacefulness of mind. That is what the whole jhana training is designed for. The sitting meditations are directly aimed at cultivating peacefulness of mind. Restlessness is thus the most targeted hindrance of the five. You are directly working against restlessness every time you're meditating.

Remorse is preventable by virtuous behavior. Virtue is a condition for samadhi, according to the suttas. Surely, it's a necessary condition, not a sufficient one (I have also encountered the opposite view). A mind troubled by remorse can hardly dwell at peace. Generally, preventing remorse will mostly be abstaining from harming or deceiving others in one way or another.

Ill will

The suttas compare a mind oppressed by ill will to boiling water.[14]

Ill will is close to anger, hate, and irritation. The classical remedy for ill will in the suttas is loving-kindness (*metta*). If you manage to replace the thoughts of ill will with thoughts of loving-kindness, it's a double win—you've overcome the

---

[13] *The Numerical Discourses of the Buddha*, sutta 5.193.

[14] *The Numerical Discourses of the Buddha*, sutta 5.193.

disturbing hindrance of ill will, and you get the benefits of a mind imbued with loving-kindness.

Anger may be easier to overcome than lust. The reason is that it's not pleasant to be angry. The cause of anger is something we dislike. The cause of lust is something we like. It's usually easier to abandon what we dislike. Lust thus tends to be more "sticky" than anger.

How do you deal with ill will, or anger? If the classical loving-kindness method works and dispels the anger, great. But it may be that it doesn't, or it works only for some time, and then the anger returns. If that is the case, loving-kindness may not be enough of a "magnet" for the mind to stick to.

Dispelling anger with loving-kindness is a specific form of replacing one thought or state of mind with another. Loving-kindness is the opposite of ill will. It is as far as you can get from it.

If you want to replace thoughts of anger with an antidote, you can think of two dimensions of the antidote you use. First, how contrasting it is to anger. Second, how well the mind sticks to it, as opposed to going back to anger—how much of a "magnet" it is for the mind.

An effective antidote to anger thus may be anything you like thinking about, as long as it's not from the unhelpful thoughts category. Something so attractive to think about that you won't tend to go back to thinking about whatever makes you angry. Ideally, it would be from the helpful thoughts category, but the neutral thoughts are acceptable too.

It may be thinking about your favorite philosophical questions, your work outside of the retreat, some "guilty pleasure" of yours, or something you look forward to. Whatever you delight in thinking about, as long as it's not associated with anger or lust. Give the mind some allowable thought candy to draw its attention away from what makes it angry. Of course, we're talking about thinking outside of meditation now.

It is using the "strongest-safe-magnet" antidote, not the opposite antidote (loving-kindness). It's not as "cool" as loving-kindness, but you don't need "cool," you need effective. Why not, if it helps forget about what causes the anger, the samadhi killer? It's not a double win, such as in the loving-kindness case, but it is a win.

It's unorthodox, I know. Some will say that the neutral thoughts are not really neutral and that you shouldn't be intentionally thinking these thoughts on a retreat. Sure. Ideally. Theoretically. But how many people can actually do that? Virtually no one— maybe some very advanced practitioners.

If you aim too high and prohibit yourself from using the neutral thoughts against anger and lust, you might end up worse off in the end. It's better to be thinking about your harmless guilty pleasures than being overcome by anger or lust. It's being pragmatic—do whatever works. But you must be honest about what works and what doesn't.

So, whenever you notice the object that stirs anger in you (usually another person) creeping into your thoughts, try to abandon it and replace it with the thought that is easy for you to stick to. Just avoid topics associated with other sources of anger or lust in any way. You can do this until the tendency to get angry subsides.

Sensual desire

The sutta simile for sensual desire portrays a mind obsessed with it as water mixed with dye.[15] Generally, it's a desire that arises on account of any of the five senses. Practically, it mainly refers to sexual desire.

The classical sutta antidote for lust is the *asubha* practice, *asubha* meaning non-beautiful, unattractive. It's done by visualizing and perceiving specific body parts (hair, skin, teeth, organs, etc.) as such. It's not that a body would be inherently ugly. A body is neither inherently ugly nor inherently beautiful. Seeing it as beautiful or non-beautiful is a matter of perception. The *asubha* practice aims to develop a perception of non-beauty to overcome lust due to the perception of beauty.

Before continuing to discuss how to deal with lust, I want to clarify the purpose of doing so. The purpose, at least in the context of this manual, is not judgmental, religious, or moral. The reason we need to overcome lust is that it excites, stirs the mind, and keeps it away from what we're trying to develop—jhana. A mind can hardly be full of passionate lust and serenely concentrated at the same time. Subduing lust is a prerequisite for entering jhana.

---

[15] *The Numerical Discourses of the Buddha*, sutta 5.193.

One may contend that going against lust is unnatural, against basic human needs. Yes, it's natural to be sexually active. And it's also natural to have an unsettled mind along with it and miss out on the benefits of jhana. Why is it that jhanas are incompatible with sexual activity? I don't know. But I can guarantee that if you do get to jhana, you will not at all regret going against lust.

As already mentioned, lust may be more difficult to abandon than anger. Lust arises based on a perception of something we find delightful and attractive, and it's associated with the potential experience of intense pleasure. There is an instinctive physical need to be sexually active, whereas there is no such physical need to be regularly angry. Overcoming the natural sexual urge is not an easy task, but it is possible, and it helps open the door to jhana.

The key to overcoming lust is creating a habit of quickly dispelling any latent thoughts associated with it. The word "quickly" is essential. The further the thoughts of sexuality unfold, the more difficult it is to stop them, and the more likely they are to arise again in the future.

I say "latent" because if you closely observe the patterns of thoughts on a retreat, you might see that the sexual craving can unfold from seemingly innocent thoughts that are not yet sexual. We can call it "undercover lust." Try to learn to identify undercover lust by observing your thought patterns.

If you find yourself thinking in the undercover lust area, try to redirect your thoughts elsewhere. It shouldn't be too difficult, as intense cravings do not yet accompany these thoughts. This is still the safe zone and the best time to act. If you miss the opportunity to abandon lust in the undercover phase, you are risking that it will unfold into a full-fledged craving. Then, you'll need much more effort to deal with it.

It's a strategy of staying as far away as possible from lustful thoughts. Whenever you sense that your thinking has the potential to develop into sexual thoughts, you move away and think about something else. The focus is on prevention so that you don't need to be extinguishing a fire later. The latent thoughts of sensuality fall into the unhelpful thoughts category—the no-no category.

So far, I have discussed only thinking. Another cause of lust arising can be perceiving our delightful object directly by the five senses. In a retreat setting, it will be mainly limited to the visual sense. Hopefully. The preventive strategy here is straightforward: avoidance. Again, I can imagine this may seem over the top to some. The reality is that avoiding visual contact, or at least minimizing it, with what stimulates lust in us—let's call it the "out of sight, out of mind" strategy—can really help. It's pragmatic and effective. Those are the strategies we want. It applies to both real-life and online scenarios.

Besides acting preventively, you need a method for quickly dispelling sexual thoughts and mental images when they do arise if the prevention doesn't hold them back. You need to find out what works best for you. If you can simply leave the lustful thoughts behind and move on—great. You may also try employing the "strongest-safe-magnet" method described earlier. A more direct way to address the issue would be the *asubha* practice. And the most radical method is probably deliberately transforming the visually attractive image in your mind into something unattractive—the "beauty is only skin deep" method.

Whichever method works best, you train to apply it as soon as the sexual thoughts arise. The sooner you manage to do that, the easier it is to stop the craving. In the beginning, it may be that nothing works well. But if you keep improving the skill of preventing and dispelling lust quickly, while developing samadhi, at some point, the lust may become weaker, it may be coming less often, and eventually, it may fade away almost completely.

Getting pleasure from samadhi helps abandon the desire for pleasure from sensuality. You don't need that sensual pleasure anymore. You have something more blissful, more profound, more fulfilling. And all you need to do is sit quietly. That is samadhi pleasure.

All in all, there is no magic pill against the hindrances. Dealing with them will always be a bit of a fight, no matter what method you use, including those mentioned above. The key to success is how you approach them, willpower, and good samadhi.

Key Takeaways

* "Developing samadhi on a retreat is the art of calming and unifying the mind in meditation and not ruining it outside of it."

* A crucial aspect of the jhana training outside of formal meditation is avoiding or minimizing the "samadhi killers." They are:

  * Using electronic devices
  * Conversations
  * Any sexual activity
  * Anger, irritation

* "The training is not meditating 24/7. During the meditation breaks, slow down, be fully aware of what you're doing— be present . . . But also relax, act normal, and smile and enjoy the process if you can."

* "The first jhana is rapture and bliss. You can hardly get there overstrained. . . . meditate as much as you can within what you can physically and mentally handle over the whole course of the retreat."

* "The key to success [in dealing with the hindrances] is how you approach them, willpower, and good samadhi."

General Meditation Tips

The following points apply to all meditations discussed in this manual.

Meditation posture

Sitting posture is crucial for meditation training. In some of the sutta sequences of successive mind qualities, what directly precedes samadhi is *sukha*, translated as "pleasure," "happiness," or "bliss."[16] The opposite of *sukha* is *dukkha*—pain, meaning pain is not at all conducive to samadhi. Pain is bad for samadhi.

Generally, the posture should be well-grounded, stable, and comfortable, minimizing pain. It should maximize the duration you can sit without physical discomfort. Full lotus, half lotus, Burmese, seiza, chair sitting . . . you need to find what works best for you. The more grounded, the better—so, the cross-legged postures are preferable to the kneeling ones, and the

---

[16] *The Numerical Discourses of the Buddha*, sutta 10.1.

kneeling ones are preferable to sitting on a chair—as long as the preferable ones are not too uncomfortable.

The posture would ideally allow you to sit still without any movements for the whole meditation session. Of course, if you need to slightly adjust the posture, such as straightening your back, that's fine. However, you should try to minimize any movements during the meditation. Also, the posture should allow you to be relaxed when meditating, not tense. Always try to be relaxed when meditating.

Combining postures

At a certain point in my practice, I wanted to increase the total time spent in meditation by combining two or even three different postures, as there is usually a limit to how long you can sit in a given posture per day. After some time, however, I realized my samadhi was not better, despite meditating longer. I don't find combining postures to increase the total time in meditation an effective way to deepen samadhi.

I suppose it's because the mind and body get used to building samadhi in a given posture, and when you change that posture, it takes some time to readjust. Changing posture slightly interrupts the momentum of the samadhi practice. The overall result, at least from my experience, is that any extra samadhi gained from the additional meditation time is not significant, and it may even have a negative effect. For example, meditating four hours a day in one posture may yield similar or even better results in terms of samadhi than meditating four hours in that posture plus two extra hours in another posture.

Still, valuing more time spent in meditation, regardless of its impact on samadhi, is also a legitimate approach. It depends on your priorities. You can experiment and stick to whatever benefits you more.

The "Lazy Lotus" posture

In the introduction, I promised to share the game-changing "trick" that helped me attain the cessation of perception and feeling. Given how crucial meditation posture is, it's no coincidence that the "trick" ended up in this section. Here is the story:

In July 2022, it had already been about three years since I managed to attain all four jhanas and four formless attainments. My primary meditation practice was being absorbed in the base of neither perception nor non-perception. Unfortunately, I've never been the most physically flexible guy. I've always struggled with discomfort in the classical sitting meditation postures. I mainly used the Burmese one. Sometimes, it was my knee, but usually it was something around my hip joint that caused the trouble. It was limiting the duration I was able to meditate without pain.

Now, you may think that there should be no perception of the body or pain in the absorption of formless attainments. So, how can I feel pain in these states? Well, it's simple—the painlessness of absorption is not limitless. If you hit someone in completely pure full absorption with a baseball bat, the meditator will experience pain, believe me. If you sit long enough, pain will creep in and "pierce" the absorption. This is what my legs were doing to my meditation.

One lucky day, the pain was coming even earlier than usual. I recalled one monk meditating in this funny posture, where he just sat on the floor with his legs stretched out in front of him and leaned back against a wall. Let's call it the Lazy Lotus posture. I was struggling enough with my Burmese posture to try it out.

After a relatively short time, my meditation went much better. Going back to the features of an optimal posture, this posture has it all for me: it's very well-grounded and stable, and all the pressure on my legs is gone. What a relief. Less pain, deeper samadhi. Easy solution.

Believe it or not, I attained the cessation of perception and feeling about three or four days later. It's hard to quantify, but if I could say a number, I would say the "ceiling" of how far I could get in meditation moved about 30–40% higher merely because I could meditate longer without physical discomfort. That was why I was suddenly able to break through into the cessation. Besides the posture change and dealing with new levels of meditation depth, I hadn't done anything differently.

I believe that had I sat like that from the beginning, I would have made it to the cessation not long after getting into the neither perception nor non-perception. I have been meditating in this posture ever since.

I'm not saying it's the best posture for everyone. But if you're one of those struggling with the classical postures due to pain, and I believe there are many people with that problem, I recommend trying it out. Some people may laugh when they see you. You may be shy to sit like that during group meditation sessions (but you don't need those to attain jhana anyway). It's not a visually impressive meditation posture, to be sure. But meditation is not figure skating. It doesn't need to look good. It needs to be good for your mind. You need the most effective posture for the mind training.

Don't let what others think limit the results of all the time and effort you put into the practice. Again, I'm not claiming it's a universally better posture than the others. It's individual. But I think it may be helpful for many meditators who've never even considered sitting like that just because "that's not how it's done." For me, it was the last missing ingredient for completing the ninefold sequence of meditative attainments.

If you try this posture, sit on something soft to maximize the time you can sit without pain. You will also need something (a folded blanket, for instance) between your back and whatever you lean against. After some time, you would probably feel pressure on the knees and heels, so you can also put something under the knees and the Achilles tendon in a way that your knees are slightly bent and the weight of your legs is not resting on the heels. Make yourself comfortable. You can adjust the set-up to relieve pain if it arises.

Where to meditate

On group meditation retreats, people usually meditate together in a meditation hall. The benefits of it can be the team spirit and that it motivates quiet sitting during the whole meditation session as you don't want to disturb others. Besides these two, I don't see any significant benefit. The other meditators will sometimes disturb you, which may not be much of a problem for insight (*vipassana*) techniques, but for developing serenity (*samatha*), a quiet place is preferable.

So, unless you find some relevant benefit in meditating with a group, the ideal setting is meditating alone in quiet, undisturbed seclusion. You can do that by holding a solitary retreat or meditating in your single accommodation on a group retreat.

How long to meditate

How long should each meditation session last? The common approach is to sit for a predefined period. I prefer a flexible duration approach. The optimal duration of a sitting session is as long as possible, within what is physically sustainable from the whole retreat perspective.

Why would you quit when still comfortably meditating? If the alarm goes off when you are still fine in your posture, you are quitting unnecessarily early. You may miss out on the juiciest part of the (unrealized) meditation. The best things can happen at the latest stages of the sitting.

On the other side, if you're painfully struggling to make it to the end of the session, you are not gaining much, if anything, in terms of samadhi, and you're increasing the chance that the physical discomfort will come even earlier in the following sessions. You are sinking yourself deeper into that physical discomfort swamp.

There comes a time in the sitting session when it becomes quite physically uncomfortable; the discomfort is not just some temporary issue—it's caused by sitting for a long time; you have the sense it's not going to get better, and it negatively affects the meditation. That is the optimal time to stop. You are meditating as long as you can while not overstraining yourself, keeping the physical sustainability of the practice in mind.

This way, the sessions can vary in duration. You don't set an alarm, but tracking each session's duration is useful. The daily schedule example has one-hour slots for sitting meditation. If you use this flexible approach, it can be less or more than that.

The downside of this flexible duration approach is that you may be indecisive about the right time to quit. Having to make that decision to stop may be a bit of a burden, but hopefully not a serious one once you get used to it.

You can experiment with both fixed and flexible duration approaches and choose the one that makes more sense to you.

Pre-play and re-play

Before every meditation session, it's good to pre-play what you want to do during the meditation. Refresh the meditation instruction from your memory, pre-play in your mind what you want to be doing, what you don't want to be doing, and how you'll react to certain situations (such as the attention wandering away from the breath during mindfulness of breathing). This mental preparation helps with executing the meditation instruction in practice.

After every meditation session, briefly re-play it in your mind. Try to understand what happened, what went well, and what didn't. Try to see patterns of how the mind works. For instance, what led to the mind being steadier? What led to the mind being distracted? Such patterns often go beyond the meditation session. Work with that too—a holistic approach. Try to leverage every relevant experience to enhance your practice. It's a learning process.

Focus on executing the instruction, not on the results

The potential danger of meditation instructions following a progressive sequence of meditative stages is that the meditator knows what is supposed to come next. It may be distracting or lead to a tendency to mentally project the next stage instead of fully focusing on the current one. Knowing what might come next is hardly avoidable. For the jhanas, specifically, whoever pursues them has likely read their descriptions before and thus has a general idea of how they might be.

Being too occupied by what could come next in meditation is a risk, indeed. But risks can be managed and mitigated. The best practice is always focusing entirely on executing the instruction for the stage you're in, to the best of your ability. It doesn't hurt to contemplate any meditative states outside of the formal meditation. However, during the meditation sessions, one should not worry about anything other than executing the instructions. Expecting specific results is never part of the instruction.

The skill to focus on executing the instruction in the present moment, instead of looking back at what happened or ahead at what may happen, is part of the mind training. If the results come, they come because you have followed the instructions, not because you have fantasized about the results.

Don't rely on your imagination and expectations about what you can or cannot do in meditation

The range of what is experienceable in meditation is difficult to imagine. It's not comparable to imagining something within our usual sensory experience. The quality, depth, and potential intensity of the nine attainments are hardly imaginable without the actual experience.

Therefore, it's not easy to describe from one side and to imagine from the other side how rewarding these states are. Also, the fact that something seems impossible to do in meditation does not mean it is impossible. It's just impossible to imagine due to the lack of any experiential reference point for such altered states of consciousness.

The point is that it doesn't make sense to give up just because one cannot imagine and lacks the confidence to get into those states. What you can or cannot imagine doing is no predictor of what you can actually do in meditation. The limit of how far the human mind can go regarding serenity is that the conscious mind activity completely ceases. There is no other way of finding out how far you can go than trying. Don't give much weight to subjective expectations about what you can or cannot attain. Such expectations can easily be inaccurate. All you can do is try your best and see what happens. The potential reward is difficult to imagine, well beyond the reward of sensual pleasures.

Extraordinary events related to meditation

Along the path of meditation, as samadhi grows, you may encounter some unusual experiences. The range of what is experienceable is vast. There are "out-of-body" experiences, experiences of nonduality, experiences of out-of-scale bliss, experiences of as if plunging into something, intense energy bursts, perceiving as if through a magnifying glass, perceiving light, perceiving only sensations in space without perceiving the borders of the body, flashes of early childhood memories, brief "cessations," which make the whole experience abruptly fall apart and reboot again, and the like.[17]

---

[17] This is only a list of what I've experienced myself. I'm sure there is more.

Such events can be very intriguing, rewarding, or even transformative. On the one hand, it will usually be an indicator of the practice going well (which doesn't mean that if you don't have such experiences, your practice is not going well). On the other hand, there is a risk of giving too much weight to it. In fact, giving too much weight to unusual experiences related to meditation is a typical source of overestimation—believing you have attained something profound while you have not. As I understand it, the extraordinary events are often nothing more than interesting by-products of samadhi.

In any case, in the context of developing samadhi, the extraordinary events shouldn't affect the practice. The instructions remain the same.

Keep your meditation techniques simple

A suitable meditation instruction is not necessarily overly complex. Its value lies in pointing the meditator in the direction leading to the desired destination. The key to progress is having an uncomplex, rightly directed meditation technique plus skillfully managing the training outside of meditation.

When you read on, you might think the formal meditation instructions are relatively few and simple. That's how it should be. A simile comes to my mind:

Suppose you're on a journey to your desired destination, but you've never walked the path before. You come to a square with several paths leading from it, not knowing which one to take. Someone comes to you and shows you a certain path, saying it leads to your destination. That advice and walking in the given direction are not at all complex (which doesn't mean that getting to the destination is easy). However, at that stage of the journey, the advice is essential. Without that relatively simple advice, you might take the wrong turns and wander for a long time without reaching your goal.

Similarly, there are many options (paths) for what you can do in meditation, most of them not leading to the samadhi attainments. The appropriate meditation instruction doesn't overwhelm you with minor details. It shows you the right direction. The simplicity of showing how to walk in that direction is not a deficiency; it reflects the nature of the practice leading to the goal.

Don't overanalyze the instructions that don't apply to you

A thing to keep in mind regarding the meditation instructions in this manual is that they are primarily meant for meditators in the given meditation stage. Due to the difficulty of imagining the samadhi states without the actual experience, the instructions can be less intuitive to those who have not yet reached the given stage. The instructions and descriptions of the states will resonate more once you're in the stage they relate to.

Key Takeaways

* "Pain is bad for samadhi. . . . meditation is not figure skating. It doesn't need to look good. . . . You need the most effective posture for the mind training."

* "The skill to focus on executing the instruction in the present moment, instead of looking back at what happened or ahead at what may happen, is part of the mind training. If the results come, they come because you have followed the instructions, not because you have fantasized about the results."

* " . . . it doesn't make sense to give up just because one cannot imagine and lacks the confidence to get into those [nine meditative] states. What you can or cannot imagine doing is no predictor of what you can actually do in meditation."

Mindfulness Training

Mindful walking

Mindful walking is a good preparatory exercise for the sitting sessions. It can settle the mind a bit, so you can get a head start in the following sitting meditation. It's also a good way to fill up your daily schedule if you have too much free time. The suggested schedule I provide includes one to two hours of mindful walking per day—30 minutes before two sitting sessions and one optional hour.

How much mindful walking you do is up to you. If you're a fan of it, feel free to do it as much as you want. It definitely doesn't hurt. A balanced approach would be doing about half an hour of walking before some sitting sessions, as the daily schedule example suggests.

Feel free to leave mindful walking out if you feel like it's not bringing much value. It's not necessary for attaining jhana.

Some mindfulness can be developed while walking, but the significance of walking is nowhere close to the sitting practice.

Mindful walking instruction

The goal is to settle the mind, cultivate mindfulness of the walking process, and stay away from restless thinking.

Three phases of a step

Find a flat straight path up to around 10 meters (33 feet) long. It's ideal to walk barefoot. Keep your eyes on the ground a few steps ahead. Walk back and forth on that path, being mindful of the three phases of each step:

→ Lifting: the foot lifting off the ground, going up in the air

→ Moving: the foot moving forward in the air

→ Stepping: the foot going down and stepping on the ground

Follow all three phases of each step. Walk in slow motion, moving one foot at a time—with the attention on the given foot, be mindful of its movement. Internally labeling the three phases of a step—lifting, moving, stepping—can help. If the attention wanders away to thinking, listening, or anything else, just realize it and bring it back to the walking process.

Walk like that to the end of the path. There, you can take a bit of a break, relax, and then turn around and go back. If you get into too much thinking during the breaks, keep them short, or just slowly turn around and go back immediately without a break.

That's it—no rocket science. Keep walking slowly, mindful of the three phases of each step for the whole session.

Five phases of a step

As you cultivate mindfulness this way, gradually, the phases may start to seem too long and too easy to follow. Then, you can split each step into five instead of three phases:

- → Raising: raising the heel off the ground
- → Lifting: lifting the foot up in the air
- → Moving: moving the foot forward in the air
- → Lowering: letting the foot go downwards
- → Stepping: touching the ground and completing the step

Everything else remains the same as for the three phases. This five-phase method is good enough to support any stage of the seated mindfulness of breathing practice.

Mindfulness of breathing (anapanasati)

The meditation technique for stilling the mind from overdrive to jhana is mindfulness of breathing (*anapanasati*). Over the course of the mindfulness of breathing training described below, the mind will, hopefully, gradually become more serene, stable, and unified around what you are mindful of. That is the development of samadhi. It can range from very mild at the beginning to the samadhi of the first jhana.

The breathing process is naturally an ideal tool for meditation. First, when you are just sitting still, breathing is the only bodily movement that remains, so it's relatively well noticeable and easy to work with. Second, it's naturally always there; you don't need to produce it artificially.[18] Third, as the mind and body affect each other, stilling the breath can help still the mind.

Combining meditation techniques

It's not uncommon to combine two or more sitting meditation techniques on a retreat instead of sticking to one at a time. An example could be supplementing the mindfulness of breathing practice with an evening session of loving-kindness or compassion meditation.

If the focus is on attaining jhana, I recommend using one technique—mindfulness of breathing—at a time. The reason is similar to not combining different meditation postures. Every time you switch from one technique to another, the mind needs to readjust. Adding another technique may thus slightly disrupt the momentum of your samadhi development effort.

However, you may become bored with mindfulness of breathing only. Adding one session of another technique in your daily schedule (perhaps shorter than the mindfulness of breathing sessions), such as loving-kindness or compassion, can gladden

---

[18] We are not worrying now about the deeper states, in which the breath subjectively "disappears."

the mind and help. But again, if you are OK without it, and your main objective is jhana, it's better to stick to mindfulness of breathing only.

I will explain three modes of *anapanasati*, where the second and third modes have two slightly different variants. An overview of the features of all the mindfulness of breathing techniques is presented in a table at the end of this mindfulness of breathing subchapter.

Mode 1: Long/short breath awareness

The sutta passage for the first mode is:

"*Breathing in long, he understands: 'I breathe in long'; or breathing out long, he understands: 'I breathe out long.' Breathing in short, he understands: 'I breathe in short'; or breathing out short, he understands: 'I breathe out short.'*" (*The Middle Length Discourses of the Buddha*, sutta 118)

The goal at this stage is to be mindful of the breath by observing whether it's long or short. As I understand it, the "long" and "short" should be interpreted as referring to the depth of breath, not the duration.[19] I also find it the more appropriate interpretation for the training. With this interpretation, a

---

[19] Just as in English, the Pali terms for *long* and *short* can refer to both time and distance. I believe the sutta speaks about how *far* the breath goes in terms of its depth, not how long it lasts.

long breath corresponds to a deep one, and a short breath corresponds to a shallow one. I stick to "long" and "short" in this manual. However, "deep" and "shallow" would be also suitable. So, you follow every in-breath and out-breath, discerning whether it's rather long (deep), or short (shallow). There are four options: long/short in-breath and long/short out-breath.

Notice that the sutta speaks about "understanding." It doesn't mention any specific location to focus on. You don't have to worry about any particular location. Try to have a general awareness and understanding of whether the in-breaths and out-breaths are long or short. You may naturally incline towards some specific area where you perceive the breath (especially if you're used to focusing intentionally on the location from your past practice). That's all right. The point is that it's not about the location. It's about being mindful of the breathing process.

You are observing the breath passively, meaning you are not intentionally influencing the breath in any way.

You can apply internal labeling. If the in- or out-breath is long, you can label it "long" (or "deep"). If it's short, you can label it "short" (or "shallow").[20] For the sake of simplicity of the labeling, you don't need to distinguish between in- and out-breath, meaning you can just use "long"/"short" for both in- and out-breath (instead of having four labeling options: "in/out long/short").

You may wonder where the threshold between "long" and "short" is. Well, it's up to you. After some time, you will have

---

[20] Of course, you can also use the corresponding terms in a different language.

a decent sample of the in- and out-breathing length (depth). Based on that, you divide the breath into what seems rather long and short. The point is to give the mind something to observe so that it stays with the breath. Exactly where you draw the line between "long" and "short" is not essential.

If you realize the mind has wandered away from the breath—you find yourself thinking, listening to something, or attending to anything else—just return your attention to the breathing process and continue. Don't see the mind-wandering as an error in the practice. It's something to work on, but not something to be frustrated about. Just keep patiently returning over and over. This approach to mind-wandering applies to all modes of the mindfulness of breathing practice.

That's it. With the help of internal labeling, try to be mindful of whether the in- and out-breaths are long (deep) or short (shallow). You do that for the whole meditation session. If it seems difficult in the beginning, and the mind is often wandering away, that's fine, that's normal. It's training the mind to be constantly with one thing only—the breath, which is not supposed to be easy. As with any other training, it requires patience, especially in the beginning.

Mode 2: Experiencing the whole body

The sutta passage for the second mode is:

"He trains thus: 'I shall breathe in experiencing the whole body'; *he trains thus: 'I shall breathe out experiencing the whole body.'"* (The Middle Length Discourses of the Buddha, sutta 118)

There are several interpretations of what "experiencing the whole body" means. For example, experiencing the whole (physical) body, experiencing the whole body (of the breath), or experiencing the whole body (through body "scanning"). I will explain the first two. They can be easily upgraded to the third mode, the gateway to the first jhana.

Experiencing the whole physical body

Don't worry about long/short anymore. Now, you're continuously experiencing, perceiving the physical body as a whole as you're breathing. If you hold your breath, it's not as easy to experience the whole body as when breathing. The breathing helps you experience the body through the movement associated with the breathing.

The breathing itself is thus not the main object of attention now. It's a tool for experiencing the physical body as a whole. In that sense, it's not mindfulness "of breathing," but rather mindfulness "of the body, while breathing." That's all right since "mindfulness of breathing" is just a specific translation of the original Pali term *anapanasati*, which may not be ideal for everything *anapanasati* refers to. I use the translation "mindfulness of breathing" because it's very common, and I'm simply going with the Bhikkhu Bodhi translations of the suttas. However, it doesn't mean that the breath is always the main object of the *anapanasati* practice.

Again, you're not necessarily focusing on any specific small location. The body as a whole is the location. You're mindful of the body as a whole throughout the entire breathing process.

You're not intentionally influencing the breathing in any way. You're passively experiencing the whole body while breathing naturally.

If the mind wanders away from perceiving the body, you just return the attention to the body and continue.

If it helps keep the attention on the body, you can continue to help yourself by internal labeling: "(whole) body." If it's unnecessary or even distracting, drop the labeling.

After some time, if the practice becomes pleasant, if it starts feeling good, that's great. Passively enjoy it, meaning let the pleasantness be there; don't try to stop it, but you're not actively focusing on it either. Treat it as nothing more than a nice by-product of the practice. You're still actively attending only to the whole body with the help of breathing.

The approach to pleasantness described above holds for all three modes of mindfulness of breathing. You can, or should, passively enjoy it but never make it your main object of attention. The task is always to follow the instructions for the given mode and treat pleasantness as a convenient by-product of the meditation. The condition for the pleasantness arising is that you have been following the instructions. Don't change the winning strategy until the mindfulness of breathing finish line (first jhana).

Experiencing the whole body of the breath

Here, you're also no longer working with the long/short breath. You're being aware, mindful of the whole breathing process from the beginning to the end (including being mindful of the gaps in between the in- and out-breaths, if they are there).

Again, it's not about a particular location of focus. It's about general awareness of breathing in every moment. It's being mindful of the fact that breathing (or the gap in between) is happening. If the mind naturally inclines towards perceiving the breath at a specific location, that's fine.

Generally, the way you perceive the breath may be naturally changing. That's to be expected—it's normal. What remains the same is the principle that you stick your attention to the breathing process and continuously follow it.

Breathe naturally. Don't try to influence the breathing in any way.

As always, if you notice the mind has wandered away, get back and continue.

If it helps keep the attention with the breath, you can again help yourself by internally labeling: "in(-breath)," "out(-breath)." If the labeling becomes redundant, abandon it.

So, the two variants of the second mode are similar. The difference is that for the physical-body one, the attention is with the physical body as a whole, and for the breath-body one, the attention is with the breathing process from the beginning to the end. You can try both variants and choose the one that feels more natural and pleasant, and during which the attention tends to wander away from the body/ breath less often.

Mode 3: Tranquilizing the bodily formation

The sutta passage for the third mode is:

"*He trains thus: 'I shall breathe in tranquillising the bodily formation'; he trains thus: 'I shall breathe out tranquillising the bodily formation.'*" (The Middle Length Discourses of the Buddha, sutta 118)

Another sutta[21] defines "bodily formation" as in-breathing and out-breathing as it is tied to the body. Other interpretations relate more directly to the physical body. The good thing is that it doesn't matter much for the practice. When you sit in meditation, the last bodily movements that still occur are those associated with breathing. Tranquilizing breathing is thus equivalent to tranquilizing the physical body.

Influencing the breath

Sometimes, it's suggested that meditation is about not "doing" anything. That "doing" in meditation is bad. For instance, the suggestion would be to always only passively observe the breath, as opposed to influencing it. Such an approach is not

---

[21] The Middle Length Discourses of the Buddha, sutta 44.

necessary. You need to "do" something in many meditation techniques. That doesn't mean you force it. You can and should still be relaxed. But you're intentionally giving a direction to what is happening.

In the first two modes of mindfulness of breathing, you only passively observe without trying to influence the breath. The point of the third mode is that you deliberately tranquilize the breathing process—the last bodily movement you can tranquilize. Whether you're coming from the physical-body or the breath-body variant of the second mode makes only a little difference. As pointed out above, stilling the breathing process and stilling the physical body are equivalent. If you're experiencing the whole body, you see it as tranquilizing the bodily movements associated with the breath. If you're mindful of the breath itself, you see it as making it as shallow as possible.

You have two tasks now. The main one is still experiencing the whole body or being mindful of the breath (depending on which second mode variant you're coming from). The additional one, in the back of your mind only, is to gradually, gently tranquilize the breath so that it (and the associated movements) becomes subtler and subtler. The limit is that it's so subtle that you can't even perceive it anymore.

The "gradually, gently" is important. If you forcefully shorten the breath, at some point, you'll need to take a deeper one to make it up and get more oxygen. That's not the way. Tranquilize the breathing body gradually, gently, and indirectly by keeping that aspiration (to still the movements or make the breath shallower) in the back of your mind. Slowly, unforcefully, you try to tranquilize as much as you can. You can try to make the breathing "disappear" (don't worry, you'll survive).

Pleasantness is your friend

The tranquilizing might make the meditation more and more pleasant. The approach to pleasantness mentioned earlier still holds. Still, take it only as a nice by-product of the practice. Do not actively focus on it. Nonetheless, at this stage, you can welcome it a bit more. You can passively delight in it. You can even smile slightly during the sitting. Meditative pleasure, happiness, and joy are conducive to the first jhana. The joy can also stem from the realization that the hindrances are gone (if they are). Allow yourself to feel happy that your mind training is going so well.

The meditative pleasantness is your friend on the way to jhana. Don't get distracted by it. Focus on walking the path. But welcome and enjoy the presence of your friend. In other words, the primary task is still being mindful and tranquilizing the breathing body, but you're also open to the pleasantness and joy stemming from the gradual unification of the mind and the weakening of the hindrances.

What if the breath "disappears"?

One "issue" that may happen at this stage is that the breath "disappears." I put "issue" into quotation marks because it's not really an issue. It's an indicator that you've been doing it right. If the task is to tranquilize the breathing, getting to the point where it's so tranquilized that you can't even perceive it is a good result. I also put "disappears" into quotation marks because, obviously, the breath never really disappears.

If the breath becomes so subtle you can't perceive it, don't see it as a problem. See it as an opportunity. When the object of mindfulness is something obvious, clearly tangible, it's easier to be mindful of it. However, subtle objects can be more conducive to getting deeper into samadhi.

If the breath "disappears," take a magnifying glass (not to be taken literally), and try to be sensitive to even the subtlest manifestations of the breath. There is a good chance you'll still be able to find something. It will require being very calm, sharp, and concentrated. You need to unify the whole mind around what you're trying to be mindful of. Calm, sharp, concentrated, mindful, unified—yes, sounds like samadhi. Working with the very subtle breath helps develop samadhi.

So, don't give up on the breath too quickly if it "disappears." It has not disappeared. It's just very subtle. Try to discern it by applying sharper, more focused attention. And if you manage to perceive that very subtle breath, keep tranquilizing even that. The instruction has not changed. You're just getting deeper and deeper.

If you really can't find the breath anymore, that's also OK. You don't need to search for some other object to work with. Being mindful of the body, or the breath, is not the purpose of the training. It's the tool you use to still and unify the mind. You can just sit there, enjoying the serenity you've developed, ready to tranquilize any subtle breathing once it appears again. It's not going to last forever. Sooner or later, the breath will be there again for you to tranquilize.

The springboard to the first jhana

A summary of the third mindfulness of breathing mode is that your main anchor is still experiencing the whole body or the breath; you have the aspiration in the back of your mind to gradually, gently, and indirectly tranquilize the breathing body by making the breath as subtle as possible; and, if it's there, you delight in the pleasantness without making it the main focus of your attention.

This technique—the third mode of mindfulness of breathing[22]—is the springboard to the first jhana. The *Anapanasati sutta* passage on tranquilizing bodily formation is followed by a passage on experiencing rapture (*piti*). Rapture is the main feature of the first jhana. From the sutta perspective, it makes sense that the tranquilizing technique would lead to jhana.

How to work with the mindfulness of breathing techniques

Outside of a retreat

Meditating 20–60 minutes daily, or at least somewhat regularly, can already make a difference. Besides the benefits

---

[22] In the sutta on mindfulness of breathing—*Anapanasati sutta*—it is listed as the fourth step, as the first two steps are covered by our first mode.

of mindfulness, it can serve as a solid basis for a potential jhana retreat in the future.

You can successively try all three modes of mindfulness of breathing, staying at least a few weeks with each. Then, you can pick the one you like the most and keep using it as your primary mindfulness technique.

In a retreat setting

If you go on a retreat and already have one of the three modes as your primary mindfulness technique, you can use it as a starting point for the retreat. If you have not yet been practicing any of the three modes described in this chapter, it would make sense to start with the first one.

This is not set in stone, but if starting with the first mode, one could switch to the second one after, let's say, five to ten days, and then to the third one after another five to ten days. This is just a suggestion. The ideal times to switch will be individual.

If one of the first two modes doesn't work well for you, you can skip it. If you have the time, eventually, it makes sense to end up in the third mode. The tranquilizing is the culmination of the pre-jhana mindfulness training. There is nowhere else to go from there in terms of developing samadhi, except for the first jhana happening.

Key Takeaways

* "Meditative pleasure, happiness, and joy are conducive to the first jhana. The joy can also stem from the realization that the hindrances are gone (if they are). Allow yourself to feel happy that your mind training is going so well. The meditative pleasantness is your friend on the way to jhana."

* "Being mindful of the body, or the breath, is not the purpose of the training. It's the tool you use to still and unify the mind."

* "A summary of the third mindfulness of breathing mode is that your main anchor is still experiencing the whole body or the breath; you have the aspiration in the back of your mind to gradually, gently, and indirectly tranquilize the breathing body by making the breath as subtle as possible; and, if it's there, you delight in the pleasantness without making it the main focus of your attention. This technique . . . is the springboard to the first jhana."

OVERVIEW OF THE MINDFULNESS OF BREATHING TECHNIQUES

TECHNIQUE FEATURES	MINDFULNESS OF BREATHING (ANAPANASATI) TECHNIQUE				
	Mode 1	Mode 2		Mode 3	
	Long/short breath awareness	Experiencing the whole body		Tranquilizing the bodily formation	
		Body variant	Breath variant	Body variant	Breath variant
Mindfulness of	Breath and its depth—long/short (deep/shallow)	Physical body as a whole	Breath	Physical body as a whole	Breath
Focus location	Not specified	Physical body as a whole	Not specified	Physical body as a whole	Not specified
Internal labeling	Recommended	Optional		Optional	
Influencing the breath	No	No		Tranquilizing	
Approach to pleasantness and joy	Welcome it, but don't focus on it	Welcome it, but don't focus on it		Passive delight; still not the main focus	
After noticing mind-wandering	Return to the main object and continue	Return to the main object and continue		Return to the main object and continue	

83

PART 2:
ADVANCED
MEDITATION

5

Jhana Training

First jhana

The timeframe for attaining the first jhana

Before discussing jhana, I must manage the expectations about the timeframe for attaining it. I want to be fair and avoid promising unlikely results. At the same time, I don't want to be too specific regarding how long it takes to attain jhana. First, it's highly individual. Second, in this regard, I myself don't know precisely where the line between possible and impossible is.

So, I will put it this way: As far as I'm aware, the most common duration of retreats is up to two weeks. You should not expect to attain jhana, even the first one, in up to two weeks of retreat. I'm not saying it's impossible. Honestly, I don't know. But it's unlikely enough that it should not be expected.

That might sound not very encouraging to some. The encouraging part, though, is that the jhana not being so easy to attain is paired with the fact that it's also quite profound. I can't imagine someone in the jhana I'm talking about saying the effort and time put into it wasn't worth it.

I want to dispel unrealistic expectations in both directions— that the jhanas are too easy or too difficult. I've suggested that one should not expect to get into the first jhana within two weeks of retreat. Let me add a hint from the other direction: Attaining the first jhana within more or less one month of retreat is possible.

Again, I'm not saying it's impossible to be quicker. I'm also not saying one month is a standard that should be expected. I'm saying that if things go relatively well—the four key factors for attaining jhana are present—the first jhana happening in more or less four weeks of dedicated practice is realistic. "The first jhana happening" is still quite far from mastering all four jhanas though.

If you only have time for retreats up to two weeks long, it doesn't mean you can't do the training. Doing the pre-jhana training—mindfulness of breathing—outside of the retreat settings, and/or occasionally on retreats of the typical duration, counts and increases your chance of making it to jhana once you do have the time for a more extended retreat. And even the pre-jhanic mindfulness states are worthwhile. It's not all only about jhana. Jhanas are the cherries on the mindfulness cake.

The typical sutta passage and simile for the first jhana are:

Here, secluded from sensual pleasures, secluded from unwholesome states, a bhikkhu [monk] enters and dwells in the first jhana, which consists of rapture and pleasure born of seclusion, accompanied by thought and examination. He makes the rapture and happiness born of seclusion drench, steep, fill, and pervade this body, so that there is no part of his whole body that is not pervaded by the rapture and happiness born of seclusion. Just as a skillful bath man or a bath man's apprentice might heap bath powder in a metal basin and, sprinkling it gradually with water, would knead it until the moisture wets his ball of bath powder, soaks it, and pervades it inside and out, yet the ball itself does not ooze; so too, the bhikkhu makes the rapture and happiness born of seclusion drench, steep, fill, and pervade this body, so that there is no part of his whole body that is not pervaded by the rapture and happiness born of seclusion.[23]

The Numerical Discourses
of the Buddha, sutta 5.28

As this is a practical manual, I will abstain from theoretical discussion of the sutta passages beyond what is necessary for describing the process of going through the meditative

---

[23] © 2012 by Bhikkhu Bodhi, *The Numerical Discourses of the Buddha.* Reprinted by arrangement with Wisdom Publications. This attribution applies to all excerpts from *The Numerical Discourses of the Buddha* throughout the manual.

attainments. An overview of the jhana practice is presented in a table following the fourth jhana subchapter.

First jhana instruction

Rapture arising

As you mindfully tranquilize the breathing body, rapture (*piti*) may arise on top of the pre-jhanic pleasantness. You don't need to try to produce it. Remember that the *anapanasati* instruction is not to focus on the pleasantness actively—not to actively try to develop it into rapture. However, rejoicing in how well the practice is going (the pleasantness, the absence of hindrances, the growing unification of mind) can help spark the rapture. It may come suddenly as an outburst, or more gradually.

I think the term "joy" is too weak for the jhanic *piti*. It's a physical rapture, ecstasy. It brightens the mind and overwhelms with energy. You may have a problem falling asleep later that night. The first surge of rapture may only last for several seconds, but the effects can be long-lasting (it wouldn't make sense to try to specify the effects' duration as you keep meditating and adding to them).

Technically, we're talking about rapture and pleasure (*piti*, *sukha*). The (mental) pleasure (*sukha*), also referred to as "happiness" in the sutta, or "bliss," is also there. At this point, however, one can hardly separate the two, and the rapture is predominant.

How do you deal with the rapture arising? Don't change anything. Not yet. Just keep following that mindfulness of breathing instruction that got you there. Treat the rapture as you've been treating the pleasantness until now—passively enjoy it as a by-product of the mindfulness training. The very nice thing about this stage is that the hindrances are gone, and you have plenty of energy and well-being for further practice.

As you keep practicing, rapture may be arising again. It may not necessarily occur in every meditation session at first. Over time, however, it might arise more frequently, earlier in the meditation session, and it may become more stable and last longer. During this stage, you're still not actively working with it.

Developing the rapture

When the rapture comes quite consistently, not only towards the end of the sessions, and is more stable, lasting longer—that is the time to adjust the technique. From now on, you're following that good old mindfulness of breathing tranquilizing instruction only until the rapture arises. When it arises, you switch, making the rapture the main object of your attention. You experience it, perceive it, enjoy it, delight and rejoice in it. That will nurture it further. Now, you do it actively. It's the main thing you do, unlike when you were just supposed to enjoy it passively.

If it fades away, go back to the tranquilizing. You start the next session again with mindfulness of breathing and switch to the rapture only when it arises. This is somewhat of a transitional period—when the rapture is there, you are with it, when it's not, you are with the third mode of mindfulness of breathing.

Hopefully, the rapture will keep developing. If it goes well, it will come consistently in every session, earlier in the sitting, and will become more and more stable. If that's the case, and you feel you already have a solid grasp on it, you can try to arouse it yourself earlier in the sitting or right from the beginning. There is no special trick for how to do that. At a certain point, the rapture and pleasure can be ingrained enough in you to arouse it with your willpower. In the same way that there is no special technique for moving your limbs—you simply have the ability to do that at will (I hope), there is no special technique for arousing the jhana factors once you've developed them enough—you can do it at will.

The ability to arouse rapture and pleasure at will allows you to abandon the mindfulness of breathing technique and switch to practicing the first jhana only. You arouse the rapture and pleasure right from the start of the sitting, and then you have only one task: maintain and nurture it by fully experiencing it, enjoying it, delighting in it. There is still thinking, and that's all right. Don't worry about the presence of thinking at this point.

Gradually, as the sutta simile depicts, you want the rapture and pleasure to pervade the whole body. You let it suffuse you entirely. You "bathe" in it. You may spread it throughout the entire body intentionally, or it might also happen naturally without much of your deliberate assistance.

Mastering the first jhana

If it goes well, you'll be able to master the first jhana. You would be able to arouse the rapture and pleasure at will, maintain it for the whole meditation session, and also exit from that state at will. The rapture and pleasure would be clear, stable, and profound, pervading the whole body. Thinking would still be there. The five hindrances should not be a problem anymore.

Second jhana

The sutta passage on the second jhana is:

> Again, with the subsiding of thought and examination, a bhikkhu [monk] enters and dwells in the second jhana, which has internal placidity and unification of mind and consists of rapture and pleasure born of concentration, without thought and examination. He makes the rapture and happiness born of concentration drench, steep, fill, and pervade this body, so that there is no part of his whole body that is not pervaded by the rapture and happiness born of concentration. Just as there might be a lake whose waters welled up from below with no inflow from east, west, north, or south, and the lake would not be replenished from time to time by showers of rain, then the cool fount of water welling up in the lake would make the cool water drench, steep, fill, and pervade the lake, so that there would be no part of the whole lake that is not pervaded by cool water; so too, the bhikkhu makes the rapture and happiness

born of concentration drench, steep, fill, and pervade
this body, so that there is no part of his whole body that
is not pervaded by the rapture and happiness born of
concentration.

The Numerical Discourses
of the Buddha, sutta 5.28

Second jhana instruction

Stopping thinking

If you have mastered and stayed with the first jhana for some time, you can continue to the second jhana. The way to do it is to stop thinking. You get into solid first jhana (i.e., wait until you get a bit deeper into the first jhana in the sitting), and then you make a deliberate effort to suppress thinking. In a similar way you would hold your breath, now you "hold your thoughts."

On the path from mindfulness to cessation, some things come spontaneously, while others do not and you need to make them happen. Stopping thinking is one of the things you need to "do." It's probably not going to be easy at first. It really requires some mental effort to make it happen. But at this stage, the first jhana mind might be powerful enough to succeed.

First, you might be able to hold your thoughts for only a few seconds. If the thinking process is really suspended during the first jhana, even a few seconds of it gives a good taste of what the second jhana is like. Keep trying to extend the time without thinking. Hopefully, the duration will gradually become longer, and it will become easier and more natural to remain in that state.

I remember I didn't believe I could stop thinking. I could not imagine how I would do that. As already discussed, it's difficult, or rather impossible, to imagine states of mind that lie outside the sphere of what we've experienced. The fact that you don't believe you can get into a certain state doesn't prevent you from getting there. Fortunately, a lack of confidence does not necessarily prevent you from progressing in meditation as long as it doesn't negatively impact your persistent effort.

For me, piercing into the second jhana was one of the most rewarding experiences on the path from mindfulness to cessation. After constantly thinking or overthinking all your life, after being entangled in the net of endless series of thoughts, you manage to stop the whole process. It's physical rapture, mental bliss, and complete inner silence and peace. Freedom from thinking. What a relief.

Developing the second jhana

You have two tasks to develop the second jhana from the initial brief periods of no thinking into mastery. First, you keep experiencing and delighting in the rapture and pleasure as you did in the first jhana. Second, you try to keep the thinking at bay and prolong the periods without it. Sometimes, you may need to focus more on the former, other times on the latter. Over time, the non-thinking will, hopefully, become effortless.

Again, as the sutta simile suggests, you let the rapture and pleasure pervade the whole body.

Mastering the second jhana

As you keep cultivating the second jhana, you might arrive at the point where you fully master it—enter it at will shortly after starting the meditation session (after sitting down, you enter the first jhana within a few seconds, and the second jhana after another few seconds), maintain it for the whole session, and exit from that state at will as well. This is already full-fledged samadhi. There is the inner silence and peace of non-thinking, the mind is well unified, firm, and stable, and the rapture and pleasure born of concentration spread throughout the whole body.

The suttas speak about the gradual stilling of verbal, bodily, and mental formations. The second jhana is the stilling of verbal formation.

Third jhana

The sutta passage for the third jhana is:

> *Again, with the fading away as well of rapture, a bhikkhu* [monk] *dwells equanimous and, mindful and clearly comprehending, he experiences pleasure with the body;*

he enters and dwells in the third jhana of which the noble ones declare: 'He is equanimous, mindful, one who dwells happily.' He makes the happiness divested of rapture drench, steep, fill, and pervade this body, so that there is no part of his whole body that is not pervaded by the happiness divested of rapture. Just as, in a pond of blue or red or white lotuses, some lotuses that are born and grow in the water might thrive immersed in the water without rising out of it, and cool water would drench, steep, fill, and pervade them to their tips and their roots, so that there would be no part of those lotuses that would not be pervaded by cool water; so too, the bhikkhu makes the happiness divested of rapture drench, steep, fill, and pervade this body, so that there is no part of his whole body that is not pervaded by the happiness divested of rapture.

The Numerical Discourses
of the Buddha, sutta 5.28

Third jhana instruction

Abandoning the rapture

When you have mastered the second jhana and kept cultivating it for some time, you can transition to the third one. The transition might come naturally and effortlessly if you've spent enough time in the second jhana. You can perceive the rapture as still being too rough, not refined enough, and you make it fade away by intentionally leaving it behind, abandoning it, dispelling it. The second jhana mind can have the capacity to do that by willpower.

When the rapture fades away, it can feel a bit "empty." The *sukha*—(mental) pleasure, happiness, bliss—is somewhat "soft" compared to the energic rapture. And as one is only starting with the third jhana, the *sukha* may be relatively subtle, not yet so tangible.

Developing the bliss

The technique for developing the third jhana is the same as for the second one. You fully experience it, enjoy it, delight in it, except you're applying it only to the bliss (*sukha*), as the rapture is gone. Not thinking should be effortless by now, so you don't need to actively focus on it anymore. And, as in the sutta simile, you let the bliss suffuse you entirely—you fully immerse in it. Gradually, the bliss should become more apparent and profound.

Mastering the third jhana

When you master the third jhana, you can enter it within a few seconds after entering the second jhana; you can maintain it for the whole session and exit whenever you want. The *sukha*—pleasant feeling, bliss—is clear and fills you up completely. Thinking and rapture are long gone. The main feature of the third jhana is the blissful feeling, which is "softer" than the rapture of the first two jhanas, yet profound. The mind is calm, mindful, unified, equanimous, filled with pure happiness.

Pleasant bliss and bliss of peace

The third jhana is the most "pleasantly blissful" state of all the nine meditative attainments. The states beyond the third jhana are neither painful nor pleasant—the feeling is neutral, which is more peaceful than a pleasant feeling, but as the definition suggests, it lacks the quality of pleasure. The third jhana is thus blissful in the sense of being profoundly pleasant, whereas the states beyond the third jhana are more blissful in the sense of being profoundly pure and peaceful without the pleasant element.

Until the third jhana, you're experiencing rapture and pleasure (*piti, sukha*) as one inseparable experience. Only in the third jhana, when you leave rapture behind and experience *sukha* alone, can you clearly distinguish the two.

Fourth jhana

The sutta passage for the fourth jhana is:

> *Again, with the abandoning of pleasure and pain, and with the previous passing away of joy and dejection, a bhikkhu [monk] enters and dwells in the fourth jhana, neither painful nor pleasant, which has purification of mindfulness by equanimity. He sits pervading this body with a pure bright mind, so that there is no part of*

his whole body that is not pervaded by the pure bright
mind. Just as a man might be sitting covered from the
head down with a white cloth, so that there would be
no part of his whole body that is not pervaded by the
white cloth; so too, the bhikkhu sits pervading this body
with a pure bright mind, so that there is no part of his
whole body that is not pervaded by the pure bright mind.

The Numerical Discourses
of the Buddha, sutta 5.28

Fourth jhana instruction

Abandoning the (pleasant) bliss

The patterns for working with the jhanas are more or less
repetitive. If you have mastered the third jhana and stayed
with it for some time, you can move on to the fourth one. The
technique for doing so is the same as moving from the second
to the third jhana, except you're abandoning the bliss of the
third jhana (*sukha*) instead of rapture (*piti*). Again, the transition
can be quite natural if you have spent enough time in the third
jhana. You can perceive the bliss of the third jhana as still being
too rough, not refined enough, and you make it fade away by
deliberately leaving it behind, abandoning it, dispelling it.

When the bliss of the third jhana goes away, the state is no
longer pleasantly blissful. What is left is an equanimous,
mindful, and pure mind without pleasure or pain. It's a bliss
of peace and purity.

Developing the fourth jhana

Developing it further into the fourth jhana mastery is similar to the third jhana. A slight difference is that since the fourth jhana lacks the pleasant element, it's less fitting to say you "enjoy and delight" in it unless it would refer to enjoying and delighting in the equanimous purity. So, you fully experience, perceive the (feeling-wise) neutral equanimous purity. You are fully with it; you immerse in it. You let it pervade you entirely, as the simile depicts. That will nurture and develop the fourth jhana further.

Mastering the fourth jhana

The result of such practice will, hopefully, be the culmination of the four jhana sequence: a mind that is exceptionally stable, unified, equanimous, mindful, pure, and bright—the pure fourth jhana mind. The suttas speak about the mind in the fourth jhana as being *"concentrated, purified, cleansed, unblemished, rid of defilement, malleable, wieldy, steady, and attained to imperturbability"* (The Numerical Discourses of the Buddha, sutta 3.58). As usual, mastering the fourth jhana means you can enter and exit from it at will and comfortably keep it going for the whole meditation session.

No breathing in the fourth jhana?

There is a sutta that says: *"For one who has attained the fourth jhana, in-breathing and out-breathing have ceased."* (The Numerical Discourses of the Buddha, sutta 9.31) In the progressive stilling of the verbal, bodily, and mental formations, this corresponds to the bodily formation being stilled, as "bodily formation" refers to in-breathing and out-breathing.

This is an opportunity to avoid falling into the trap of taking everything in the scriptures literally. If people in the fourth jhana were literally not breathing, they would soon be brain dead, of course. As I understand it, the sutta refers to the breath becoming so subtle that it "has ceased" from the meditator's perspective. As discussed earlier, the breath "disappearing" can happen even during the mindfulness of breathing practice. The breath in the fourth jhana is so subtle that the meditator doesn't perceive it, but physiologically, there is still breathing.

OVERVIEW OF THE JHANA PRACTICE

	JHANA			
	First→	Second→	Third→	Fourth
E N T E R I N G ↓	Rapture (*piti*) and pleasure (*sukha*) arising	Stopping thinking	Abandoning the rapture (*piti*)	Abandoning the pleasure, bliss (*sukha*)
D E V E L O P I N G ↓	Experiencing, delighting in the rapture (and pleasure); pervading the whole body with it	Same as the first jhana + prolonging the periods without thinking	Experiencing, delighting in the pleasure, bliss (*sukha*); pervading the whole body with it	Experiencing, perceiving the equanimous purity; pervading the whole body with a pure bright mind
D E V E L O P E D	Rapture (and pleasure) clear, stable, profound, pervading the whole body; thinking present; hindrances gone	Same as the first jhana, except the thinking is gone—inner silence and peace	The pleasure, bliss (*sukha*) clear, stable, profound, pervading the whole body; rapture gone; a mindful, equanimous, happy mind	The equanimous purity clear, stable, profound, pervading the whole body; pleasure, bliss (*sukha*) gone; a mindful, equanimous, pure bright mind

Notes on practicing the four jhanas

Jhanas as progressive refinement by abandoning

After getting into the first jhana, in a way, going through the jhanas is refining the mind by abandoning. By abandoning thinking, you get to the second jhana. By abandoning rapture, you get to the third jhana. And by abandoning pleasure, you get to the fourth jhana.

That's all true. It's also important to add, though, that the abandoning requires developing the rapture and pleasure in the first place, and the whole process requires very solid samadhi. Without mentioning this, the jhanas might sound too easy, as if it all were only about leaving something behind. That would be incomplete and inaccurate. Going through the jhanas is a constant mind development, which involves dropping some of the jhana factors along the way—that's what gets you from one jhana to another. However, abandoning on its own is not the whole picture of the jhana practice.

Going up and down the jhana sequence

Mastering more than one jhana means being able not only to go up the jhana sequence but also down. There is no special trick for doing so. The mind that masters the jhanas has the ability to turn the determining jhana factors—rapture, thinking, pleasure—on and off at will. In that sense, going up the sequence means:

→ rapture (and pleasure) ON—first jhana
→ thinking OFF—second jhana
→ rapture OFF—third jhana
→ pleasure OFF—fourth jhana

Going down the sequence from the fourth jhana then means:

→ pleasure ON—third jhana
→ rapture ON—second jhana
→ thinking ON—first jhana
→ hindrances ON— . . . just kidding, don't turn those on . . .

Where in the body are the jhanas experienced?

The jhanas are whole-body experiences. Going through the meditative attainments, I was often surprised by how physical these states were. Nevertheless, the main thing always clearly happens in the head. Developing the jhanas for the first time felt like an almost constant "adjustment" of something in the head. One of the main experiential features of developing each jhana was something like an "evolving pleasant pressure" in a specific location in the head (a different location for each jhana). When the jhana developed and stabilized, the evolving pressure dissolved, and how the jhana felt in the head also stabilized.

The timeframe for attaining all four jhanas

To anchor the expectations regarding the timeframe for going through all four jhanas, let's say that if things go very well, it's possible to do it within three months of retreat. Again, I'm not claiming it's impossible to be faster. I'm also not saying that getting into all four jhanas in three months is a standard. I'm saying that if things go very well and the key factors for attaining jhana are fulfilled, it's not impossible to do it within three months.

By three months of retreat, I don't necessarily mean the most intense retreat, meditating constantly all day. But I do mean a set-up where the meditator is dedicated full-time to the on- and off-the-cushion training, quite secluded, and meditating several hours a day (such as in the daily retreat schedule example provided earlier).

Benefits of the jhanas

I'm unaware of any adverse side effects of the jhanas as described in this manual. Naturally, the most direct benefit is being in those profound states in meditation. In addition to that, the benefits experienced outside of the formal meditation are many:

- As the mind is serene and mindfulness pure, the working patterns of the mind are more visible. The jhanas are an ideal base for developing insight (*vipassana*), whether in or outside of formal meditation. Wisdom gained by seeing things as they really are is the primary purpose and potential benefit of samadhi from the Buddhist perspective.

- There is calmness of thoughts and more control over them. If you want to think about something, you can. If you don't want to think about it, you don't. You have a choice. There is no obsessive thinking, no restlessness, no uncontrollable inflow of thoughts. I see this as one of the top benefits.

- As the jhanas are primarily experienced in the head, a certain "feel" stays there beyond the meditation sessions. It's not easy to describe. To use a few words, I would say it feels very pleasantly light, soft, and smooth in the head (each jhana having its own distinctive "flavor" of it). That is my subjective description. I suppose other meditators might describe it using different words. In any case, I consider it one of the most tangible and rewarding effects of the training. Compared to the normal states of mind without jhana practice, the head is in constant comfortable bliss.

- The mind is composed, stable, and equanimous, far from stress, anxiety, and emotional instability.

- The body is relaxed, with less tension and pain. You can also sit longer in meditation as samadhi reduces pain perception.

- The mind is bright and fresh, and the body is energized. You hardly get drowsy.

- Falling asleep is blissful and easy (except if the mind is too bright and energized from meditation), and you wake up into pleasantness, well rested and refreshed. Dreams are peaceful and more often recallable.

- There is no craving for sensual pleasures. You get plenty of well-being from the jhana bliss instead.
- Memory and concentration improve.
- One notable benefit of deep jhana practice I've experienced is that it completely silences tinnitus[24]. Without deep samadhi, I constantly hear a mild buzz. It's not too bothersome. Maybe it's quite normal. The beautiful thing is that with deep samadhi, it's completely gone (even outside of the meditation sessions). You can enjoy both inner and outer silence.

The benefits above are only those directly experienceable. There are likely additional health benefits not noticeable right away (and I will leave that topic to the scientists).

---

[24] A condition when you hear a sound, such as ringing or buzzing, without any external source.

Key Takeaways

* "Doing the pre-jhana training—mindfulness of breathing—outside of the retreat settings, and/or occasionally on retreats of the typical duration [up to two weeks], counts and increases your chance of making it to jhana once you do have the time for a more extended retreat.... It's not all only about jhana. Jhanas are the cherries on the mindfulness cake."

* " . . . in a way, going through the jhanas is refining the mind by abandoning. By abandoning thinking, you get to the second jhana. By abandoning rapture, you get to the third jhana. And by abandoning pleasure, you get to the fourth jhana.... It's also important to add, though, that the abandoning requires developing the rapture and pleasure in the first place, and the whole process requires very solid samadhi.... abandoning on its own is not the whole picture of the jhana practice."

* [One of the jhana benefits experienced outside of the formal meditation:] "There is calmness of thoughts and more control over them. If you want to think about something, you can. If you don't want to think about it, you don't. You have a choice. There is no obsessive thinking, no restlessness, no uncontrollable inflow of thoughts."

Beyond Jhana:
Formless Attainments

If you've mastered the fourth jhana and have more retreat time ahead, you can try to go beyond the fourth jhana to the formless attainments. As mentioned in the Theory chapter, the key difference between the four jhanas and the formless attainments is absorption (also described in the Theory chapter). The formless attainments are close to the fourth jhana in that they feel neither painful nor pleasant—neutral. The fourth jhana and the formless attainments are also all called "imperturbable" in the suttas. The additional feature of the formless attainments is absorption with a single fixed perception (neither perception nor non-perception in the case of the fourth formless attainment).

The "borders" between the different formless attainments are less robust than those between the four jhanas. The transitions from one formless attainment to another are correspondingly smoother. It's "only" moving from one perception to another subtler perception, whereas in the case of the jhanas, the various jhana factors come into play. Once you manage to get to the base of infinite space, there is a good chance that going through the four formless attainments will be less time-consuming than going through the four jhanas.

The suttas are rather concise on the formless attainments. The passage for the transition from the fourth jhana to the first formless attainment—base of infinite space—is as follows:[25]

" . . . *with the complete surmounting of perceptions of form, with the disappearance of perceptions of sensory impact, with non-attention to perceptions of diversity, aware that 'space is infinite,' we enter upon and abide in the base of infinite space."* (*The Middle Length Discourses of the Buddha*, sutta 31)

Explanation of the formless

The formless as temporary liberation

A bit of theory and explanation is needed to make sense of the "formless." In the context of the early Buddhist texts, meditative experience can be either within form (*rupa*) or formless (*arupa*). It's also translated as material (*rupa*) and immaterial (*arupa*). The four jhanas fall into the sphere of form as one in the jhanas is still experiencing form, matter (*rupa*), although in a very refined, agreeable way. Since *rupa*, in general, is considered to be associated with suffering

---

[25] It's the same passage as in the Theory chapter.

(the suffering arising on account of existing in the physical, material world), transcending it, going beyond it into *arupa*—the formless—is considered liberation, although temporary. In this context, it's "only" liberation from *rupa*, not the final liberation of Nirvana. As the sutta passage suggests, one can do that by surmounting perceptions of form, sensory impact, and diversity, and entering the base of infinite space.

By the way, some call the four jhanas "rupa-jhanas" and the formless attainments "arupa-jhanas." This manual sticks to the suttas, which never call the formless attainments "jhanas."

From getting absorbed to the edge of perception

There are two formless elements in the sutta context: space and consciousness.[26] After surmounting perceptions of form and getting into the first formless state—infinite space—the next step is surmounting that base of infinite space. When one accomplishes that, what's left is a perception of infinite consciousness. After surmounting the perception of infinite consciousness, as there is no more formless element to perceive, only a perception of nothingness remains. The meditator still fully perceives at that point, but the "object" is nothing. It's an experience of nothingness, but it's still an experience.

Surmounting that perception of nothingness gets you to the edge of perception—a state called "neither perception nor non-perception." It's not enough of a perception to call it "perception,"

---

[26] *The Numerical Discourses of the Buddha*, sutta 3.61.

but it's not yet cessation of perception. It's something in between. While for the base of nothingness, you can say you're perceiving nothingness, for the neither perception nor non-perception, you can't really say what you're perceiving. It's a sort of residual perception of nothing identifiable.

Why is it that the brain can produce these states? Don't ask me—I don't know. But the amazing thing is that these states of mind really exist, and getting there is doable with the key factors for developing samadhi fulfilled.

One thing I want to clarify is that, in the context of meditation, when we speak of the "base" of infinite space, infinite consciousness, nothingness, or neither perception nor non-perception, it does not refer to some special existential dimension or anything like that. The infinite space, consciousness, and so on, are real in the sense that it's really what the meditator vividly experiences and perceives. But it's not real in the sense that the meditator would be entering some "realm" of infinite space, consciousness, and so on. The formless attainments are nothing more, nothing less than self-induced, deeply absorbed altered states of consciousness with a single fixed perception (as opposed to perceptions of diversity)—of infinite space, infinite consciousness, nothingness, plus the state of neither perception nor non-perception.

Formless means formless

Some things in the suttas are to be taken literally, some are not (and yes, then the million-dollar question is which is which). The formless attainments are to be taken literally. For example, infinite space after surmounting perceptions of form, sensory impact, and diversity really means just infinite space, nothing else. It doesn't have any other quality than being an empty space that is infinite, boundless (but, of course, we can say the state of mind as such is peaceful, serene, imperturbable, and the like). It's neither beautiful nor repulsive, neither painful nor pleasant—it's just space. If the meditator experiences any other qualities, such as colors, sounds, flavors, whatever, then it's not the formless infinite space or any other formless attainment.

Infinite space

Getting absorbed

"Upgrading" from the fourth jhana to the formless infinite space—absorption—is one of the things you need to work on deliberately. It's not going to come spontaneously.

You get into the fourth jhana and imagine empty space all around, everywhere—nothing else than boundless space in all directions. It's an imagination, a mental projection. With the fourth jhana as a base (which should be very well established by now), you keep developing a perception of infinite space all around.

In the beginning, it might not be working very well. The projection won't seem very real at first. This phase requires some patience. However, as the fourth jhana mind is malleable,[27] gradually, the projection can become more and more "real."

Occasionally, internally labeling what you're trying to project— "(infinite/boundless) space"—can help. It technically violates the purity of the jhana (there is no verbal mental activity from the second jhana onwards), but if it helps with the mental projection, it's OK. Infinite space is the priority now.

Try to fully immerse in that emerging perception of infinite space. The mind will be less and less percipient of all other things. The meditation may also be getting more and more gratifying; not in the sense that there would be pleasant feelings, but in the sense that the samadhi becomes more peaceful, more detached from the external world.

The process of getting absorbed is neither purely gradual nor all at once. It's a combination of both. The process above— the meditator being less and less percipient of anything else than the increasingly real perception of infinite space—is gradual. However, there is a specific moment when the mind finally gets fully immersed as if soaked in or locked into the experience of infinite space. The perception of infinite space thus becomes clear and complete, filtering out all other experiences, including sensory perceptions. That is full absorption, the attainment of the formless infinite space, temporary liberation of the mind from matter.

----

[27] See Mastering the fourth jhana in the Fourth jhana section of chapter 5.

Switching to the autopilot

Entering absorption is the time to switch to "autopilot" mode. From now on, there is not much to actively do. The only task is to keep going forward experiencing, perceiving infinite space without actively being in charge of what is happening.

To some extent, that is already the case in the jhanas. The absorption brings it to another level. In absorption, any move of the attention away from the infinite space (or the other formless bases) gets the meditator out of the absorption. In jhana, the field of attention still compatible with the jhana is broader. The formless states thus require a higher level of detachment. Detachment from everything, including the intuitive tendency to have a sense of control over what is happening with the mind, except the given formless base.

Don't try to check for absorption

There might be a tendency to check if you're really absorbed—if there is no sensory perception. Such a check doesn't work. The senses are not impaired. They are fully functional. The absorption just filters out the sensory experience. If you intentionally try to check if there is hearing, meaning you pay attention to any sounds, there will be hearing. If you try to check whether you're experiencing the physical body by switching attention to it, you will experience it. The checking itself will always get you out of the absorption. All one can do is, after the meditation session, look back and evaluate whether there was a period of absorption. So, don't worry about checking for absorption during the meditation session. It doesn't work, and it only interrupts the absorption.

Delight in release and detachment

As already pointed out, the autopilot mode requires letting go of being in charge. There is a natural tendency to try to be in control of what is happening. This shouldn't be surprising. That is more or less what we do our whole lives. You can consider the autopilot mode a training of letting go, abandoning, releasing. Try to develop the habit and mindset of delighting in the sense of letting go, abandoning, releasing, detachment. Let the samadhi get in charge. Just enjoy the serenity of infinite space. That will work best and develop the state further. Well-developed absorption then has the nice "locked-in" feature that makes staying in it easier and more natural than getting out of it.

Infinite consciousness

" . . . by completely surmounting the base of infinite space, aware that 'consciousness is infinite,' we enter upon and abide in the base of infinite consciousness." (The Middle Length Discourses of the Buddha, sutta 31)

From space to consciousness

After mastering the base of infinite space, one can transition to the base of infinite consciousness. As noted earlier, the "border" between the two states is relatively subtle. Getting deeper into the infinite space state can lead to spontaneously entering the base of infinite consciousness. The perception of space disappears, and the mind is left with a perception of infinite consciousness.

If it doesn't happen spontaneously, the technique is in principle the same as for moving from the third to the fourth jhana. You can perceive the space as still too rough, not refined enough, intending to move on towards something even more subtle, refined, and peaceful—such as infinite consciousness. And you deliberately relinquish the perception of infinite space.

As the perception of infinite consciousness is more refined than that of infinite space, it's even more gratifying. Generally, for all the attainments, the higher it is, the more rewarding it gets.

The term "consciousness" can have slightly different meanings in different contexts. This is also the case in the suttas. In the context of the second formless attainment, the meaning of "consciousness" is close to that of "mind." The meditator is experiencing nothing but a formless infinite mind. The other features of the absorbed state and the way to develop it deeper remain the same as for the infinite space.

Interpreting infinite consciousness

Once again, I want to make clear that experiencing infinite consciousness/mind does not refer to something overly metaphysical. Being absorbed in infinite consciousness/mind doesn't mean "being one with universal consciousness" or something like that. Meditative experiences are always subject to interpretation. If you put people who firmly believe in universal consciousness or something similar into the base of infinite consciousness I'm talking about, they might interpret it as "merging with universal consciousness." I don't interpret it that way. As I see it, the formless attainments are extremely valuable and fulfilling meditative experiences for the meditator. But their meaning doesn't go beyond that in the sense that they would have some externally metaphysical element.

Nothingness

" ... by completely surmounting the base of infinite consciousness, aware that 'there is nothing,' we enter upon and abide in the base of nothingness." (The Middle Length Discourses of the Buddha, sutta 31)

From consciousness to nothingness

For the base of nothingness and how to work with it, everything is the same as for the infinite consciousness, except the perception changes. Only a perception of nothingness is left after the infinite consciousness vanishes. It's a perception of absence of a thing, a perception of voidness, emptiness.

Nothingness as emptiness

Attaining the formless nothingness should not be mistaken for the Buddhist practice of perceiving things as empty.

From the Buddhist perspective, everything has the inherent quality of being empty of an unchanging, permanent entity or core. That is the "non-self" (*anatta*)—the cornerstone of the Buddha's teaching. Seeing, perceiving, or contemplating *anatta* is a practice of developing insight—*vipassana*, whereas being in the formless base of nothingness—that is, perceiving that state's emptiness—develops serenity—*samatha*. The point of the former is understanding the *anatta* nature of things, whereas the point of the latter is the stillness of mind.

Neither perception nor non-perception

" . . . *by completely surmounting the base of nothingness, we enter upon and abide in the base of neither-perception-nor-non-perception*." (*The Middle Length Discourses of the Buddha*, sutta 31)

From nothingness to the edge of perception

Again, working with the base of neither perception nor non-perception is the same as for the preceding formless attainments.

As noted earlier, there is only residual perception in the neither perception nor non-perception, and you can't tell what it is that you're still residually perceiving. This state is different from the preceding three in that those three are defined by their perception, whereas this fourth one is defined by its lack of perception ("neither perception"), while not yet being the cessation of perception ("nor non-perception"). My experience is that it also takes longer to fully develop compared to the other three formless states.

The most serene conscious state available

According to the suttas, this is the highest conscious meditative state possible. It's the most peaceful conscious state available. Beyond that is only the cessation of perception and feeling—an unconscious state. The neither perception nor non-perception is extremely blissful because of how serene it is. Indeed, all the lower attainments are too rough, not refined enough, in comparison.

Working with the eight meditative states

Going down the attainment sequence is a nice-to-have

Mastering the eight meditative attainments (four jhanas plus four formless states) means not only being able to go up the sequence but also down. However, besides being a nice skill to have, going down the sequence doesn't have much practical use. The main meditation base will likely be the highest attainment the meditator can reach (I don't see much reason for that not being the case). Even if you decide to stay in one of the lower attainments of your samadhi repertoire, you do that by going up there and not going further up the sequence. And you can always end the meditation session by opening your eyes in whatever state you're in. You don't need to go back down to the first jhana to end the session. So, in no usual scenario, does one need to go down the sequence of the meditative attainments.

Focusing on the highest attainment you can get into

If the objective is getting as far as you can in the sequence of attainments, focusing on developing the highest one you can get into is most effective. After starting the meditation session, you can go up the sequence to your highest attainment as quickly as your ability allows you. There is no need to stay in a lower attainment longer than what is necessary to get into the next one, a higher one. That applies to the lower attainments you have mastered in the past. Developing a particular state into mastery and then moving on to the subsequent attainment is a different thing, which should not be rushed through.

The scale of depth and the "grey" area

If well developed, going up the jhanas and the formless attainments might be a matter of a few seconds. But that needs further clarification. The meditative states, except for the cessation of perception and feeling, are not a "0/1" thing. The reality is more fluid than that. Within what technically qualifies as jhana or a formless attainment, there is a scale of depth one can get into. In addition to that, there can be a grey, hybrid, or impure area, in which the state does not technically qualify as jhana or a formless attainment, but it's much closer to it than to anything else.

So, for example, when I say you can get into the fourth jhana within a few seconds, that means you can get into a decent level of the jhana quickly (which can still be very deep in absolute terms), and only after some time meditating, you get into your deepest fourth jhana.

Similarly, for the formless absorptions, you may be able to quickly get into a state that closely resembles the formless attainment, is not yet full absorption (therefore, doesn't qualify as a pure formless attainment), but is much closer to the pure formless absorption than to anything else. Let's call it "pre-absorption." And only after some time of meditation, you deepen it into complete absorption.

So, to be more precise, if you become skillful in the formless attainments, it will probably mean being able to get quickly into that pre-absorption state, while still needing some more time to get fully absorbed into what qualifies as a pure formless attainment.

Key Takeaways

* "Since *rupa* [form], in general, is considered to be associated with suffering (the suffering arising on account of existing in the physical, material world), transcending it, going beyond it into *arupa*—the formless—is considered liberation, although temporary. . . . As the sutta passage suggests, one can do that by surmounting perceptions of form, sensory impact, and diversity, and entering the base of infinite space."

* " . . . there is a specific moment when the mind finally gets fully immersed as if soaked in or locked into the experience of infinite space. The perception of infinite space thus becomes clear and complete, filtering out all other experiences, including sensory perceptions. That is full absorption, the attainment of the formless infinite space, temporary liberation of the mind from matter."

* "There is a natural tendency to try to be in control of what is happening. . . . Try to develop the habit and mindset of delighting in the sense of letting go, abandoning, releasing, detachment. Let the samadhi get in charge. . . . That will work best and develop the state further."

Cessation of Perception and Feeling (Nirodha Samapatti)

. . . by completely surmounting the base of neither-perception-nor-non-perception, we enter upon and abide in the cessation of perception and feeling. . . . There is no other comfortable abiding higher or more sublime than that one.

The Middle Length Discourses
of the Buddha, sutta 31

Venerable sir, what is the difference between one who is dead and gone, and a bhikkhu [monk] who has attained the cessation of perception and feeling?

Householder, in the case of one who is dead and gone, the bodily formation has ceased and subsided, the verbal formation has ceased and subsided, the mental formation has ceased and subsided; his vitality is extinguished, his physical heat has been dissipated, and his faculties are fully broken up. In the case of a bhikkhu who has attained the cessation of perception and feeling, the bodily formation has ceased and subsided, the verbal formation has ceased and subsided, the mental formation has ceased and subsided; but his vitality is not extinguished, his physical heat has not been dissipated, and his faculties are serene. This is the difference between one who is dead and gone, and a bhikkhu who has attained the cessation of perception and feeling.[28]

The Connected Discourses
of the Buddha, sutta 41.6

Explanation of the cessation

As for the four preceding formless attainments, the name of this final stage of the ninefold attainment sequence simply says what the state is about—cessation of perception and feeling. Along with perception and feeling, consciousness also ceases. It is to be taken literally. The whole conscious experience shuts down. The meditator doesn't have any experience of the cessation period. You can't be conscious of consciousness

---

[28] © 2000 by Bhikkhu Bodhi, *The Connected Discourses of the Buddha.* Reprinted by arrangement with Wisdom Publications.

having ceased. The meditator only experiences the moments before and after the cessation.

Unconsciousness is an inherent feature of the cessation of perception and feeling. However, unconsciousness itself doesn't imply the cessation, of course. The two terms are not always interchangeable. Thinking of the meditative cessation only as unconsciousness would be too much of a simplification. The way to induce the cessation unconsciousness and its effects on the body and mind are unique to that state, as far as I'm aware, distinguishing it from other types of unconsciousness. In any case, in the context of this chapter, when I speak about the absence of consciousness, I'm referring to the cessation of perception and feeling.

As the sutta above suggests, the difference between a dead person and a meditator in the cessation of perception and feeling is basically that the mental processes have ceased in both cases, but the meditator remains physiologically alive.

However, the meditator is not entirely "cut off." Some intense external stimuli (pain, sounds) can interrupt the cessation. This means the mind-body in the cessation is still sensitive to an intense sensory impact on an unconscious level. The cessation is a deeply detached unconscious state, but not to the point of the meditator being completely "unwakeable."

"Mental formation" refers to perception and feeling in the suttas.[29] The cessation of perception and feeling thus completes the progressive stilling of the verbal, bodily, and

---

[29] *The Middle Length Discourses of the Buddha*, sutta 44.

mental formations. The ninefold sequence of the meditative attainments gradually stills the mind to the point where it turns off completely. Processes like thinking and perceiving via the five senses are "switched off" along the way.

By definition, the cessation of perception and feeling is the highest attainment possible in terms of serenity (*samatha*). The mind cannot be more serene than being "turned off." There is nowhere further to go in terms of calming the mind.

Three tips for attaining the cessation

1. Give it a try

"You miss 100% of the shots you don't take."

Wayne Gretzky, Michael Scott

The first and most crucial tip is straightforward: try.

Surely, the cessation is a very high goal. The highest meditative goal. It requires months or years of full-time dedicated mind training. Generally, it will be realistic only for those who can put together the four factors for developing samadhi to a higher degree.

Nevertheless, it's not as impossible as many people think. There is a widespread belief in the Theravada tradition that the cessation of perception and feeling is accessible only to those with the qualities of an *anagami* or an *arahant*—the two highest stages of enlightenment in the early Buddhist texts. Believe it or not, it's not true. You don't need to be an *anagami* or an *arahant* to attain the cessation.

Some, or maybe many, will not accept that claim. That's fine. To those who are willing to believe it and have the conditions and motivation to try: go for it. It's doable and worth it. In this manual, I'm sharing the most relevant information I'm aware of that might help you make it.

2. "Program" the mind to shut itself down

The second tip is the technique for stilling the mind all the way to the cessation.

The theory is not complicated: you're in the neither perception nor non-perception, and you need to keep stilling the mind further until it shuts down. More specifically, in the neither perception nor non-perception, there is still some subtle mental activity going on. It's mostly the residual perceptions and volitions—intentions. For example, there can be the intention to exit from the state at the end of the session. Or there can be the intention to keep doing what you're doing— just going forward in the autopilot mode. Despite the state being relatively very serene, there are some subtle mind moves arising. Only the cessation is free from that. To enter it, you need to still even the subtlest mind-moves.

What is the trick for doing so? What is the technique? Well, there is not much discretion to do something. You're deeply absorbed, very much in the autopilot mode. However, it's also not 100% passive. It's not that you have zero influence on what is happening in the mind. There is some discretion in setting the course for the autopilot. You can "program" the autopilot to go in a certain direction.

When you practice (the third mode of) mindfulness of breathing, the technique can be something like: "Keep experiencing the whole body; also, gradually tranquilize the breathing process; if the mind wanders away, get it back; if it becomes pleasant, (passively) delight in it . . . ." The technique for getting from the neither perception nor non-perception to the cessation can't be that elaborate. It can't be keeping multiple objectives in mind. It can't be "If this happens, I do that; if another thing happens, I do something else." There is no room for that in such a deeply absorbed state.

You need one very simple rule for that small amount of discretion you have there, for those occasions when you're not only passively following through. That rule should "program" the autopilot to go in the direction of stilling all mental activity. Also, it needs to be applicable to anything arising in the mind. It needs to be universal and simple.

The golden rule

The rule is to cut, abandon, relinquish anything that arises in the mind. Any subtle mind move that arises in the mind, anything happening in the mind beyond just going forward in the autopilot mode—you cut it, abandon it, don't let it unfold immediately as it arises. It doesn't have the nature of forcing it out. It has the nature of releasing it.

You apply it to anything arising, even to the intention to follow this rule itself. If the intention to cut whatever arises in the mind arises in the mind, you cut that intention as well (of course, without abandoning the whole practice of cutting whatever arises in the mind). At that point, it becomes strangely paradoxical, but it works.

So, you're either entirely in the autopilot mode, just going with the flow (that will likely be most of the time), or you're applying this rule. In other words, you are either "doing nothing" or using the rule. The rule is the universal reaction to anything happening in the mind beyond the autopilot.

You develop the rule into a habit. You program the mind to release any subtle mind activity arising. That is the directing of the autopilot towards the cessation—*nirodha samapatti*. Gradually, it can become natural and automatic. This is the mind mode that can lead the mind to shut itself down.

3. Double down when fear arises

Fear could pose a challenge at this stage of the path—the fear of losing control and the fear of the unknown.

It shouldn't be surprising. You're getting to the borders of conscious experience. You're close to turning your consciousness off. It's hard to imagine someone attaining the cessation experiencing absolutely no fear beforehand. In fact, fear arising is an indicator that the practice is going well. It means you are getting closer to the goal, which lies outside of your known comfort zone.

The main issue may not be the thing causing the fear itself but that it surprises you, and you shy away. Getting familiar with the states bordering on the cessation helps. Seeing that nothing bad ever comes out of it, that there is nothing to be afraid of, the fear may gradually subside.

Use your pre-play

Generally, a more active way of dealing with fear is working with it in your pre-play. The fear is usually caused by some extraordinary event[30] in meditation that drags the meditator out of the known comfort zone. The extraordinary events can also be the most valuable ones—if you don't turn away and you go through them.

So, you get mentally ready for it in your pre-play. You realize that the fear might arise, that it's an indicator of the practice going well; you can actually see it as a window of opportunity arising, and you determine not to shy away but to double down instead should it arise—you will steadily go against the fear, following through whatever is causing the fear as far as you can. Courage pays off.

---

[30] The extraordinary events were discussed in the General Meditation Tips chapter.

This "if-then" rule can be an exception to having only the one golden rule described earlier (the fear arising is an exceptional event, rather than a standard part of meditation).

My first experience of emerging from the cessation

I say "experience of emerging" because the cessation itself is never experienced. "Experience of the cessation" is an oxymoron unless it refers more broadly to the experience including the moments before and after the cessation, which are the only parts consciously experienced.

The first emerging from the cessation has been by far the most intense experience I've ever had. The extraordinary thing about the first emerging was its overwhelming physical impact. Two similes came to my mind shortly afterward: as if struck by lightning or hit by a truck (not that I've ever experienced either of the two). The initial main impact was brief, let's say a few seconds. It was an intense overwhelming shock wave originating in the head, going through the spine, and impacting every inch of the body. The intensity was outright frightening and shocking, yet the effect was calmingly blissful. There was a quick flash of bright white light in the mind (although it was literally enlightening, it wasn't "the enlightenment"—experiencing light doesn't make you any more enlightened). It felt like a breaking of a barrier. No emerging from the cessation ever since has felt that intense.

At first, I tried to keep meditating. After a short while, I gave up. I was too overwhelmed by what happened, so I opened my eyes. Deeply calming bliss was pervading my body, and I was staring in front of myself in shock. The mind reached another level of serenity and brightness, even compared to the already very serene and bright mind of the formless attainments.

I kept staring there in front of myself, probably for a few minutes, being shocked by the event's intensity. After a while, I burst into tears. It was not like there was a choice. It felt like an unstoppable physiological reaction to the shock.

Right after the initial intense event, I thought it was the cessation. But it doesn't come with a label "cessation of perception and feeling." Some verification wouldn't hurt. I will discuss later in this chapter how to check whether the cessation is happening.

Some of the features and effects of the cessation practice

The subjective continuity of experience

Theoretically, it might be obvious, but in reality, it can still be somewhat unintuitive: The overall cessation experience, including the period before and after it, is subjectively 100% continuous. There is zero sense or memory of any gap, of any interruption in one's conscious experience—the cessation. Subjectively, all you get is the moments before the cessation immediately followed by emerging from the cessation. So, the cessation causes a sudden switch from the mind before to the mind after it, while in fact, the mind before and after the cessation can be separated by a fair amount of time.

The continuity was also somewhat surprising to me the first time I went through the cessation. All there was was the extraordinary experience I described, with no sense of any gap, no sense of the cessation itself. Again, theoretically, it makes total sense, and it can't be otherwise. Yet it can be unintuitive in practice, especially in the beginning.

The difficulty of knowing the cessation duration

All you can do regarding estimating the cessation duration is deduct the time you remember being aware from the total time of the meditation session. The tricky part is, of course, that remembering how long you were aware is subjective and may not be accurate, especially in such deep meditation, where time subjectively goes by faster. Nonetheless, if you're well familiar with how, let's say, one hour of the neither perception nor non-perception is, you can make a reasonably reliable estimate of how 20 or 30 minutes of it is. They're always only estimates, but they can be legitimate if you try to be as objective as possible and don't fall into self-deceit.

With only one long cessation within a meditation session, estimating the duration would be relatively easy. That's already a very advanced practice, however. More likely, there will be several cessations within one meditation session. In that case, you can estimate the duration of all the cessations together but not the durations of the individual cessations (unless you would disturb yourself by pressing a stopwatch button after emerging from each cessation). I estimate my longest overall cessation duration to be 30–40 minutes within one hour of meditation.

If the cessation practice is not yet well developed, and you attain it only now and then for a short time, it's virtually impossible to know the duration. That was the case with my first cessation. The emerging from the cessation came towards the end of a meditation session that didn't appear to be significantly shorter than what the stopwatch showed, meaning it may have been anything from a few seconds to a few minutes. There is no way to find out.

Nonduality

By nonduality, I mean that the subject-object perspective of experiencing subsides. It's no longer "I experience something." Instead, it's "an experience is happening" with no or less of a sense of the "I." Experiencing becomes impersonal.

Continuous practice of the cessation of perception and feeling generates, prolongs, and intensifies nondual awareness both during the meditations (speaking of the periods when you're aware, not in the cessation) and outside of them.

Generally, nondual experiences can vary in duration and intensity. They can be intense to the point of being frightening.

The fear is caused by the sense of losing one's "self." In such cases, the strategy of doubling down and going against the fear applies. Selflessness is the limit (and, unlike experiencing light, 100% selflessness is the enlightenment—Nirvana—according to the Buddha's teaching).

Dreamless sleep

Practicing jhana can result in more frequent and vivid dream recall. After some time of the cessation practice, on the contrary, sleep becomes strikingly dreamless.

How to check if the cessation is happening

To prevent overestimation, a down-to-earth assessment and critical thinking are essential. There is no perfect self-check for the attainment of *nirodha samapatti*. However, checking for it can be relatively more reliable than for the lower meditative attainments.

For any non-cessation meditative attainment, you need to judge whether the quality of your experience matches how the attainment is defined. The tricky part is, of course, that interpreting meditative experiences is subjective. Different meditators can interpret different experiences similarly and similar experiences differently.

For the cessation, the situation is more straightforward. The attainment is defined as the mental formation—perception and feeling—ceasing. The meditator's state, or "experience," is compared to that of a dead person, the difference being that the meditator is still physiologically alive. The cessation is a non-experience.

So, the test is whether the mind is "on" or "off." You're judging whether there was a period during which you were unconscious. It's a "0/1" test for a period of unconsciousness. Such a test is relatively easier and more objective than evaluating whether your experience matches certain non-cessation qualities.

There is no hard proof of the cessation. It's rather a combination of indicators that can point to it:

Cessation indicators

The intensity of the first emergence

This is the necessary condition even to consider the possibility that the cessation happened.

Sure, one could object that the emerging from the cessation may not be the same for everyone. I agree. And I admit I have a tiny sample size of how the first emergence is. However, based on the experience I had and the fact that it's supposed to be the highest meditative attainment possible according to the suttas, I would be very surprised if the breakthrough into it would be a mild event for anyone. Within the field of samadhi experiences, the intensity should probably be a multiple of anything you have experienced before, including the most intense experiences of the jhanas and the formless attainments. It should be a big outlier. A hypothesis as to why that might be the case is outlined in the next chapter.

The intense experience I describe is not hard proof of *nirodha samapatti*. However, I think it's a valid indicator. The formless attainments, and the neither perception nor non-perception especially, are very consistent states. One of the main features is their stability. Yes, there are still some little changes. There are still some subtle mind moves. But there are no sudden intense "roller coasters." None.

In that sense, the hypothesis that such an intense experience would be "nothing," or some part of the neither perception nor non-perception state, is more challenging to uphold than the hypothesis that, indeed, it is emerging from the cessation of perception and feeling. There are no explanations more rational and consistent with the nature of the formless attainments than the experience being emergence from the cessation.

But, of course, that is sort of a "What else would it be?" indicator, which doesn't work with the absence of perception, feeling, and consciousness. It inherently assumes that the cessation is what follows what I call "neither perception nor non-perception." So, let's move on to the indicators based on the absence of perception, feeling, and consciousness, which have more objective strength.

The missing time indicator

This is the most obvious indicator. It relates to what I've discussed regarding the difficulty of knowing the cessation duration. Suppose a significant amount of time is "missing" from the meditation session, and it's accompanied by the experience(s) unusual to the neither perception nor non-perception that seems to be the emergence(s) from the cessation. That might be an indicator of the cessation.

The issue is the subjectivity of time perception. That is why "significant" (amount of time missing) is essential. For instance, if the meditation session lasts 80 minutes and feels like only an hour, it doesn't mean that much. It's not unusual that meditation feels somewhat shorter than how long it actually is according to the stopwatch. But if you're well familiar with how 80 minutes of the neither perception nor non-perception is, and it suddenly seems to be, let's say, shorter by half or more, that can already be a cessation indicator.

The light switch indicator

Upon emergence from the cessation, the experience is briefly as if the mind is collecting back together, and the mind may not be fully absorbed. Still with the eyes closed, it's possible to perceive whether it's dark or light outside. Also, it's possible, or rather quite likely, that there are multiple cessations within one meditation session, not just one. The cessations can follow shortly after each other. Combining all that with meditating from darkness to daylight in the morning, or daylight to darkness in the evening, can serve as a cessation test.

In the case of the morning, for example, if the meditation session covers both when it's still dark outside and when it's light, you might experience one emergence from the cessation, being aware it's still dark outside, shortly after that followed by another emergence from the cessation, being aware of daylight outside. It can be almost like turning on the light switch. It can be going from complete darkness to full daylight in a few moments, while in reality it obviously takes more time. That indicates the mind was really "turned off" between what you consider to be the two emergences from the two cessations.

The missing movement indicator

The cessation subjectively works as a bit of a time machine—in an instant, you move forward by the cessation duration, which can be a few seconds, several minutes, or longer. In addition to that, the upper torso and the head might slightly move during the cessation without interrupting it. From the meditator's perspective, due to the continuity of experience, the result is that the position of the head instantaneously switches from A to B with absolutely no sense of the movement from A to B. If the first emergence from the cessation was the most intense meditative experience I've ever had, this may be the weirdest one. It feels very strange—like an instantaneous fast-forwarding into a different time and position.

This is only a passive indicator. The moving during the cessation may or may not happen. So, if you never experience it, it doesn't imply there is no cessation. If it does happen, though, it can be another piece of the puzzle indicating that, indeed, there was a period when you were unconscious.

The impossibility of checking for short cessations

The last three indicators are all based on a sufficiently long period of non-experience occurring. No such indicators are available for brief cessations (that still perfectly qualify as *nirodha samapatti*, no matter the duration). All the meditator has is the mind quickly changing from the mind before to the mind emerging from the cessation, which can be a more or less profound experience (except for the very first emergence, which should be exceptionally profound). But there is no way to self-check that a short time is missing from one's experience. All you have is what you consider to be the emerging from the cessation, which is basically the mind suddenly changing in some way. But the mind quickly changing is not that unusual. That can happen even for non-cessation events.

What does it mean? It doesn't mean that claims of short cessation attainments should be outright dismissed. It does mean, though, that such claims are solely based on the meditator's belief that what is happening is the entering and emerging from the cessation, without any at least somewhat objective evidence of the mind being really "turned off." The lack of evidence is not the fault of the meditator, however. It's impossible to have such evidence for brief cessations, even if they're real.

Making a fact-based judgment

So, first, you may be confident you have attained *nirodha samapatti* based on the quality and intensity of the believedto-be first emergence from it, accompanied by the profound effects it has beyond the meditation.

Then, you might be able to support that initial confidence by the indicators pointing to the mind being shut down for sufficiently long periods.

And, finally, by then, you know how emerging from the cessation is, so you can also identify the short cessations by it, despite not having any bulletproof self-check for them.

Overall, there is no scientific-level cessation self-check available for the meditator. However, with the approach outlined above, critical thinking, and resistance to self-deceit, it's feasible to make a reasonably reliable judgment whether the cessation of perception and feeling is happening. In any case, the judgment should be fact-based, not driven by wishful thinking and bias.

Key Takeaways

* "The rule [to attain the cessation] is to cut, abandon, relinquish anything that arises in the mind [while in the neither perception nor non-perception]. Any subtle mind move that arises in the mind, anything happening in the mind beyond just going forward in the autopilot mode—you cut it, abandon it, don't let it unfold immediately as it arises. It doesn't have the nature of forcing it out. It has the nature of releasing it. . . . This is the mind mode that can lead the mind to shut itself down."

* " . . . the overall cessation experience, including the period before and after it, is subjectively 100% continuous. There is zero sense or memory of any gap, of any interruption in one's conscious experience—the cessation. Subjectively, all you get is the moments before the cessation immediately followed by emerging from the cessation."

* "Continuous practice of the cessation of perception and feeling generates, prolongs, and intensifies nondual awareness both during the meditations (speaking of the periods when you're aware, not in the cessation) and outside of them."

General Notes

Delight in an ever more refined form of bliss is the fuel of progress

The ninefold sequence of meditative attainments is a step-by-step refinement from a more or less restless mind to temporary cessation of all mind experience. What is being delighted in also refines along the way. For the mindfulness of breathing, it's the pre-jhanic pleasantness. For the jhanas, it's the jhana factors, mainly the rapture and pleasure. For the formless attainments, it's the serenity of absorption—a refuge from sensory impact. And for the cessation of perception and feeling, it's the sense of abandoning, release, detachment—that is the most sublime delight of all.

The common feature of all the stages is having a good time in your meditation. Don't hesitate to enjoy it. The more enjoyable it is, the smoother the progress. The ever more refined form of bliss *is* the progress.

Normalization and the contrast effect

For all nine meditative attainments, subjective normalization of how it "feels" works, both in and outside of the meditation (for the cessation, only outside). The more you experience the contrast in terms of the meditation's depth, the more intense the experience appears.

The most gratifying are usually the phases of progressing deeper in meditation. When you settle in a particular state and maintain it, after a while, it may not seem as impressive as when you were progressing towards it. You get used to it. It becomes the new normal. The benefits of the meditation remain, no doubt. The nine states are always very rewarding. The phases of progressing deeper just usually have an extra kick to them.

The contrast effect works downward as well. If you settle in a certain state, it normalizes, and only when the samadhi weakens, for example, due to meditating less (such as when you're writing a meditation manual), will you be reminded how relatively deep and fulfilling that earlier state was.

As I understand it, the contrast effect is also at least partially responsible for how intense the first emergence from the cessation is. It's directly experiencing the contrast between the mind before and after the first breakthrough into *nirodha samapatti*. The following cessations may be longer, yet emerging from them is not as intense because the contrast between the before and the after is not as profound. It's no longer the breaking of a barrier. This is the hypothesis for why the first emergence is so unique in its intensity.

Overestimation

"The first principle is that you must not fool yourself—and you are the easiest person to fool."[31]

Richard Feynman
Nobel Prize-winning physicist

Self-deceit is not your friend. Generally, overestimation—believing you have attained something while you have not—is a common pitfall in meditation. It's pretty easy to overestimate oneself due to the subjectivity of interpreting meditative experiences. It can be very tempting. All you need to do is to conclude that whatever you experienced is whatever you had been striving for, and that's it—there are your "results." The convenience of concluding one has attained something and the lack of objective checks for it is a tricky combination. Overestimating is a risk deserving careful attention.

It wouldn't make sense to talk about overestimation without establishing what we consider to be jhana. The potential overestimation depends on how you interpret the attainment. I explained earlier in the manual which interpretation of the jhanas and the other attainments this manual works with.

---

[31] Richard Feynman, "Cargo Cult Science," commencement address at California Institute of Technology, Pasadena, CA, June 14, 1974.

Adopting a different interpretation of the meditative states could change the conclusion about overestimation.

Here are a few thoughts and tips on how to avoid overestimation:

Exceptional states in meditation do not imply jhana

Overestimation is related to the difficulty of describing and imagining how the jhanas are. The path of samadhi is a progressively more refined form of bliss. From mindfulness to cessation, it gets better and better. The result is that every time you reach the new highest point in your meditation, it's the "best meditation ever," and it may not be easy to imagine how it would get much better than that.

"The best meditation ever" is very relative though. It's easy to think like that about the pre-jhana states, and you would also think like that after emerging from *nirodha samapatti*. And it's usually hard to imagine how it would get much better because it's simply impossible to accurately imagine how far the mind can go before it actually gets there.

The point is that "the best state ever" in meditation does not yet imply it's jhana. It may or may not be. There are undoubtedly non-jhana altered states of consciousness that can feel awesome.

Critically evaluate three aspects of the practice

So, how do you recognize jhana? Besides discussing it with a more samadhi-experienced meditator, the best you can do to

check for any meditative attainment is to critically evaluate
three things:

1. During the meditation, are all the qualities that are
    supposed to be present in the mind for the given state
    really there?
2. During the meditation, is the mind really free from
    what is supposed to be absent in the given state?
3. Outside of the meditation, are you experiencing the
    benefits of the jhanas?

For example, there is no first jhana without evident (physical)
rapture, no second jhana with internal verbal activity present,
and no formless attainments with sensory perception. And if the
mind still gets easily restless, drowsy, lustful, irritated, or the
like outside of the meditation, whatever you're experiencing,
it's probably not jhana.

All three aspects of the practice should be critically evaluated.
Concluding that you've made it to the given state should follow
only after answering "yes" three times to the questions above.

Don't tailor your jhana interpretation to your own meditation

Being so eager to attain, the mind can tend to seek for any
experience that may qualify as a success. That itself is natural
and not necessarily a big issue. The problem starts when
evaluating whether the meditative experience matches the
attainment description becomes too flexible, driven by the
desire for accomplishment.

It can go so far that the mind starts adjusting the meaning of the attainment description to fit one's own experience. It can lead to quite creative interpretations of the attainments. Don't fall for it. Don't try to tailor what the jhanas mean to your own experience. It's OK to overestimate. Everyone makes mistakes. But if we want to be serious about the practice, we should be honest with ourselves, and the evaluation should be as fact-based, rational, and unbiased as possible.

Being honest means going with the interpretation one thinks has the highest chance of being the true meaning of jhana after at least some basic research into the topic, not going with the interpretation that works "best" because it's closest to one's own meditation experience. I recommend doing at least basic research into the historical development of Buddhism and the corresponding traditions, scriptures, and practices.

Being aware that the mind can tend to seek anything confirming the attainment and accept alternative interpretations of the jhanas in order to achieve "success" can help prevent overestimation.

Don't blindly believe others

Another source of overestimation can be believing a teacher who, for whatever reason, calls something "jhana" that is not jhana. There is only one way to prevent that: Don't blindly believe anyone—do your own research, use your own brain. Teachers can be easily wrong, no matter their renown.

Underestimation

Underestimation is also a thing. However, due to the relatively high standard of how the nine states are interpreted in this manual, it shouldn't be much of a problem. Only if you see the four jhanas as full absorptions and enter what this manual calls jhana would you not see it that way, and thus underestimate from the perspective of this manual's standards. Besides that, I can hardly imagine someone going through any of the nine states described here and concluding that it's not enough to qualify for the attainment.

Drawing conclusions

If your meditation feels great and special but doesn't pass the critical evaluation test to qualify for jhana, that should not at all be a discouragement. Quite the contrary. It's a good sign. It might be signaling talent for samadhi and good practice. It can be an encouragement to prolong the retreat and progress further in samadhi, hopefully, all the way to jhana, which will feel even better. Remember that the range of meditative bliss is vast and difficult to imagine until it's actually experienced.

If your meditation does pass the critical evaluation and has all the features of jhana, it's legitimate to conclude it's jhana. The assessment shouldn't be biased in either direction. Try to be careful not to overestimate, but you don't need to be intentionally overskeptical either. After all, what matters most is the effects of the meditation, not the label you put on it.

Remain open to adjusting past conclusions

Generally, all you can do to avoid overestimation is try to make a well-informed rational judgment about whether what is happening in your meditation constitutes jhana and be open to adjusting your past conclusions if you realize they've been inaccurate. Being mistaken is not as much of a problem as the potential unwillingness to see it, admit it, and fix it. The jhanas are great, and the honesty of admitting not getting there is great too. Self-honesty and truth-seeking is the best long-term strategy.

Key Takeaways

* "The common feature of all the [meditative] stages is having a good time in your meditation. Don't hesitate to enjoy it. The more enjoyable it is, the smoother the progress. The ever more refined form of bliss *is* the progress."

* "Self-deceit is not your friend. Generally, overestimation—believing you have attained something while you have not—is a common pitfall in meditation.... The convenience of concluding one has attained something and the lack of objective checks for it is a tricky combination. Overestimating is a risk deserving careful attention."

* "Being mistaken [i.e., drawing inaccurate conclusions about your meditation] is not as much of a problem as the potential unwillingness to see it, admit it, and fix it. ... Self-honesty and truth-seeking is the best long-term strategy."

Conclusion

The jhanas are not easy. Just reaching the first jhana is a huge meditative success that only some meditators will achieve. The good news is that understanding the determinants of success—the key factors for attaining jhana—enables working more effectively toward fulfilling the three of the four you can influence. That's the purpose of this manual—to help make jhana training as effective as possible. Effort alone, even if persistent, is not enough. Trying harder doesn't always imply better results. To bear fruit, the effort needs to be smart and rightly directed.

In this manual, I've shared the most relevant "tips and tricks" I'm aware of for developing samadhi from the most basic practice of mindfulness of breathing, through the four jhanas, all the way to the cessation of perception and feeling (*nirodha samapatti*)—the highest meditative attainment possible according to the early Buddhist scriptures. It combines an ancient tradition (the meditative states are based on texts dating back over 2,000 years), a pragmatic analytical approach, and practical knowledge gained through personal experience with all the meditative states discussed, not learned from any book or scripture.

The fact that formal meditation instructions do not take up the lion's share of the manual illustrates the importance of everything surrounding the formal meditation techniques. It's a holistic approach.

I wish all those on the path of meditation a smooth journey from mindfulness toward the utmost peace of cessation.

What you can do, or dream you can, begin it.
Boldness has genius, power, and magic in it.

Johann Wolfgang von Goethe[32]

---

[32] Paraphrased by John Anster. For details, see *Quote Investigator*, February 9, 2016, https://quoteinvestigator.com/2016/02/09/boldness/.

Summary of Key Takeaways

Introduction

* "This manual provides comprehensive practical guidance for developing the jhanas (profoundly serene and blissful states of meditative concentration), potentially all the way to the cessation of perception and feeling (*nirodha samapatti*)—the highest meditative attainment possible according to the early Buddhist scriptures."

* "The manual focuses on mind training in a retreat setting, covering both the time on and off the meditation cushion."

* "The manual is suitable for anyone (laypeople, monks, or nuns) aspiring to go beyond basic mindfulness on a meditation retreat."

PART 1: GROUNDWORK FOR SERENITY

1. Theory

* " . . . of the three types—let's call them 'lite,' 'intermediate' and 'absorption' jhanas—the jhanas I talk about are closest to the intermediate type."

* "Exactly that [absorption], as I understand it, is the main difference between the four jhanas and the formless attainments. The four jhanas are not absorption, while the formless attainments are."

* "Cultivating samadhi is going beyond mindfulness, but it doesn't mean you leave mindfulness behind. Mindfulness is highly developed in the jhanas. . . . If you want the purest mindfulness, go for the jhanas."

* The four key factors for attaining jhana are:

  • Favorable external (retreat) conditions
  • Good instruction and advice
  • Persistent effort
  • Talent

* "Don't focus on things you cannot control, such as the results. Focus on things you can influence, such as your persistent effort."

2. Training Outside of Meditation

* "Developing samadhi on a retreat is the art of calming and unifying the mind in meditation and not ruining it outside of it."

* A crucial aspect of the jhana training outside of formal meditation is avoiding or minimizing the "samadhi killers." They are:

  • Using electronic devices

- Conversations
- Any sexual activity
- Anger, irritation

* "The training is not meditating 24/7. During the meditation breaks, slow down, be fully aware of what you're doing—be present . . . But also relax, act normal, and smile and enjoy the process if you can."

* "The first jhana is rapture and bliss. You can hardly get there overstrained. . . . meditate as much as you can within what you can physically and mentally handle over the whole course of the retreat."

* "The key to success [in dealing with the hindrances] is how you approach them, willpower, and good samadhi."

3. General Meditation Tips

* "Pain is bad for samadhi. . . . meditation is not figure skating. It doesn't need to look good. . . . You need the most effective posture for the mind training."

* "The skill to focus on executing the instruction in the present moment, instead of looking back at what happened or ahead at what may happen, is part of the mind training. If the results come, they come because you have followed the instructions, not because you have fantasized about the results."

* " . . . it doesn't make sense to give up just because one cannot imagine and lacks the confidence to get into those [nine

meditative] states. What you can or cannot imagine doing is no predictor of what you can actually do in meditation."

4. Mindfulness Training

* "Meditative pleasure, happiness, and joy are conducive to the first jhana. The joy can also stem from the realization that the hindrances are gone (if they are). Allow yourself to feel happy that your mind training is going so well. The meditative pleasantness is your friend on the way to jhana."

* "Being mindful of the body, or the breath, is not the purpose of the training. It's the tool you use to still and unify the mind."

* "A summary of the third mindfulness of breathing mode is that your main anchor is still experiencing the whole body or the breath; you have the aspiration in the back of your mind to gradually, gently, and indirectly tranquilize the breathing body by making the breath as subtle as possible; and, if it's there, you delight in the pleasantness without making it the main focus of your attention. This technique . . . is the springboard to the first jhana."

PART 2: ADVANCED MEDITATION

5. Jhana Training

* "Doing the pre-jhana training—mindfulness of breathing—outside of the retreat settings, and/or occasionally on retreats of the typical duration [up to two weeks], counts

and increases your chance of making it to jhana once you do have the time for a more extended retreat. . . . It's not all only about jhana. Jhanas are the cherries on the mindfulness cake."

* " . . . in a way, going through the jhanas is refining the mind by abandoning. By abandoning thinking, you get to the second jhana. By abandoning rapture, you get to the third jhana. And by abandoning pleasure, you get to the fourth jhana. . . . It's also important to add, though, that the abandoning requires developing the rapture and pleasure in the first place, and the whole process requires very solid samadhi. . . . abandoning on its own is not the whole picture of the jhana practice."

* [One of the jhana benefits experienced outside of the formal meditation:] "There is calmness of thoughts and more control over them. If you want to think about something, you can. If you don't want to think about it, you don't. You have a choice. There is no obsessive thinking, no restlessness, no uncontrollable inflow of thoughts."

6. Beyond Jhana: Formless Attainments

* "Since *rupa* [form], in general, is considered to be associated with suffering (the suffering arising on account of existing in the physical, material world), transcending it, going beyond it into *arupa*—the formless—is considered liberation, although temporary. . . . As the sutta passage suggests, one can do that by surmounting perceptions of form,

sensory impact, and diversity, and entering the base of infinite space."

* " . . . there is a specific moment when the mind finally gets fully immersed as if soaked in or locked into the experience of infinite space. The perception of infinite space thus becomes clear and complete, filtering out all other experiences, including sensory perceptions. That is full absorption, the attainment of the formless infinite space, temporary liberation of the mind from matter."

* "There is a natural tendency to try to be in control of what is happening. . . . Try to develop the habit and mindset of delighting in the sense of letting go, abandoning, releasing, detachment. Let the samadhi get in charge. . . . That will work best and develop the state further."

7. Cessation of Perception and Feeling (Nirodha Samapatti)

* "The rule [to attain the cessation] is to cut, abandon, relinquish anything that arises in the mind [while in the neither perception nor non-perception]. Any subtle mind move that arises in the mind, anything happening in the mind beyond just going forward in the autopilot mode— you cut it, abandon it, don't let it unfold immediately as it arises. It doesn't have the nature of forcing it out. It has the nature of releasing it. . . . This is the mind mode that can lead the mind to shut itself down."

* "... the overall cessation experience, including the period before and after it, is subjectively 100% continuous. There is zero sense or memory of any gap, of any interruption in one's conscious experience—the cessation. Subjectively, all you get is the moments before the cessation immediately followed by emerging from the cessation."

* "Continuous practice of the cessation of perception and feeling generates, prolongs, and intensifies nondual awareness both during the meditations (speaking of the periods when you're aware, not in the cessation) and outside of them."

8. General Notes

* "The common feature of all the [meditative] stages is having a good time in your meditation. Don't hesitate to enjoy it. The more enjoyable it is, the smoother the progress. The ever more refined form of bliss *is* the progress."

* "Self-deceit is not your friend. Generally, overestimation—believing you have attained something while you have not—is a common pitfall in meditation. . . . The convenience of concluding one has attained something and the lack of objective checks for it is a tricky combination. Overestimating is a risk deserving careful attention."

* "Being mistaken [i.e., drawing inaccurate conclusions about your meditation] is not as much of a problem as the potential unwillingness to see it, admit it, and fix it. . . . Self-honesty and truth-seeking is the best long-term strategy."

Acknowledgments

My gratitude goes to all the good people who supported me along the path of meditation, directly or indirectly, including all the devotees of the Sasanarakkha Buddhist Sanctuary in Malaysia.

Special credits go to Gautama Buddha, the Blessed One, the Revealer of the path to cessation; my dear teacher Venerable Ariyadhammika Mahathera, who taught me a large part of what I share in the manual, whose wisdom and tireless patience with his disciples are exemplary; and my family for always being there for me.

References

Bhikkhu Bodhi. *The Connected Discourses of the Buddha.* Wisdom Publications, 2000.

— *The Numerical Discourses of the Buddha.* Wisdom Publications, 2012.

Bhikkhu Bodhi, and Bhikkhu Ñāṇamoli. *The Middle Length Discourses of the Buddha.* Wisdom Publications, 2009.

Sparby, Terje, and Matthew D. Sacchet. "Toward a Unified Account of Advanced Concentrative Absorption Meditation: A Systematic Definition and Classification of Jhāna." *Mindfulness* 15 (2024): 1375–1394. https://doi.org/10.1007/s12671-024-02367-w.

Van Dam, Nicholas T. et al. "Mind the Hype: A Critical Evaluation and Prescriptive Agenda for Research on Mindfulness and Meditation." *Perspectives on Psychological Science* 13 (2017): 36-61. https://www.researchgate.net/publication/320317493.

Yates, John, Matthew Immergut, and Jeremy Graves. *The Mind Illuminated: A Complete Meditation Guide Integrating Buddhist Wisdom and Brain Science for Greater Mindfulness.* Atria Books, 2017.

*If you found this manual helpful and wish to learn more or support this work, visit **www.jhana.training***

Made in the USA
Las Vegas, NV
24 June 2025